DUCK DUCK GROOM

●

UNDERSTANDING
HOW A CHILD
BECOMES A TARGET

●

ANNA SONODA, LCSW

ISBN: 979-8-218-03199-2
Library of Congress Control Number 2022913309

The information presented is the author's opinion and does not constitute any mental health or medical advice. The content of this book is for informational purposes only and is not intended to diagnose, treat, cure, or prevent any condition or disease. The advice and strategies found within may not be suitable for every situation. Care has been taken to ensure the information in this book it true and correct at the time of publication. The author assumes no liability of any kind with respect to the completeness or accuracy of the contents. The author cannot be held liable or responsible to any person or entity with respect to any loss or incidental or consequential damages caused by or alleged to have been caused directly or indirectly by the information herein. Please seek advice from your behavioral health provider for your mental health concerns prior to taking advice from this book.

Names, characters, places and events either are the product of the author's imagination or are used fictitiously for education only. Any resemblance to actual persons, living or dead, events or locales are entirely coincidental.

Cover: Blake C. Tannery, Bravo Charlie Tango
Book Design: Blake C. Tannery, Bravo Charlie Tango

First printing, 2022.

Anna Sonoda, LCSW
1800 Peachtree Street, Suite 430
Atlanta, Ga 30309

www.annasonodalcsw.com

For Dale!

Ann Sandler

DEDICATION

To you, the reader, because through you, this world can change.

ACKNOWLEDGEMENTS

This book is the biggest professional undertaking of my life and I met incredibly talented people in my pursuit to publish. Firstly, my sincerest thanks to my developmental editor, Sarah Mac Smith. You energized this project wholeheartedly and gave me the assignments and accountability necessary to make it come true. Thank you for meeting me at the YMCA, at the house with a crying baby spitting up on my shoulder, and virtually anywhere I asked. You'll be my first call for the next one.

Next, thank you, Jennifer Goode Stevens, for your time and talent to copy edit this manuscript. Your suggestions and perspective were on point. You were my clean set of eyes when my vision blurred and I'm thankful for your help. Hopefully, we will meet in person one day in Nashville.

To the tremendous Blake Tannery for your graphic design work and formatting. Blake, you're talented beyond belief and I'm in awe of your ability to make my words seen. Thank you for immaculately designing the cover for this book. Nikki was right; you're the best out there.

To my beta readers and opinion givers, thank you for telling me honestly how to improve this manuscript. Special thanks to Kelly, Amy, Kristy, Brittany and Denise. To Fiona, my best friend and favorite sister, thank you for caring about and improving this project. Seriously.

To my parents who were ever-present cheerleaders for this book idea. What more can a daughter ask for than the two of you. I love and respect you immensely. Thank you for believing I could do this.

To my children, my vocation, thank you for being the music to this dance of life.

Saving the best for last, to my one and only. Thank you falls ridiculously short of expressing all the ways you have championed this book and my dreams. You're my treasure.

CONTENTS

PROLOGUE

Nine years ago, I experienced what I can only describe as a type of possession. A spirit took over my mind and heart, blaring a recurring message: "Share what you know." But what I knew was hard to share, so I looked for any excuse to avoid responding to this call. Parenting my young children kept me plenty busy, but running did not quiet the deafening gong. So I finally started writing. It wasn't much at first, but slowly the words started falling onto the pages, and the spirit and I were able to work together. With the help of my supportive family, friends, and brave editors, this book—my mental exorcism—took shape.

This book is about a tough subject. As a licensed clinical social worker, I worked in a treatment setting where we provided individual and group cognitive behavioral therapy for convicted sex offenders. While completing my degree, and then for another few years, I met with individuals, couples, and groups each week—discussing topics relevant to their sexual crimes, their reentry into society, and their personal relationships. Later, after I had my first child, the experience of working with these sex offenders stayed with me. All those conversations about child abuse were etched in my mind, and have informed nearly every decision I've made as a parent ever since.

Just thinking about child sexual abuse sends panic through most parents. Horror stories about child molesters make some parents worry to the point of paranoia. Afraid they cannot keep their children safe, they limit their children from age-appropriate, safe, and fun activities where the children could grow and learn. For other parents, the reality of the risks is too awful to consider. Sadly, they stick their heads in the sand and fail to head off the dangers, just hoping everything will somehow be okay. If I hadn't worked with sex offenders, I might have been no different. But during my time inside those rooms, I learned something I don't think enough parents know: It is easier than most people realize to protect a child from sexual predators.

My Reassuring Discovery

The most important lesson I learned from listening to sex offenders is that there is a clear lead-up to child sexual abuse, and it is gradual, intentional, and observable. If you educate yourself on these grooming strategies and are willing to look for them, you can spot the warning signs and prevent abuse long before it has a chance to begin. You can also structure a child's life and activities in ways that make it difficult, or impossible, for grooming to start.

The overwhelming majority of abused children—more than 90 percent[i]— know their abusers; they have an existing relationship before the abuse begins. These predators follow the predictable, courtship-like pattern that we call grooming, which requires a period of at least days or weeks— usually months, and sometimes years. Grooming involves not just the child, but also anyone responsible for the child, and it is how a molester gains enough access to sexually abuse a child.

The caring adults who keep children safe can encounter multiple chances to cut off a predator's access to a child, especially if they recognize grooming when they see it. When a child suffers abuse, people often look back and see a path littered with these opportunities, missed. The grooming routine is relentlessly predictable. Those of us who have worked with sex offenders know it all too well, having heard the end result again and again. My hope is that by shining a light on it, we can spare at least one child, one family the devastation that all too often follows the grooming process.

I have written this book so that you can know the routine, too, and be alert to any attempts at grooming that may happen around you. Knowledge is power, and by knowing what to look for, you gain the power to protect your child and other children around you from being victims of sexual predators. Learning about grooming patterns enables you to connect your parental instincts with research-backed strategies to reduce the abuse risk for the children you know. Combining this knowledge with the ability to distinguish instinctive fear from panic will be your best approach. There's no need for panic or paranoia, as both are counterproductive. What you need instead is education about grooming—plus a habit of steady, careful attention.

Anyone, Anywhere

Another lesson I learned working with sex offenders is sobering: These predators can be anyone, anywhere.

I've never forgotten my first day on that job as a social worker. When I opened the door to our waiting room, the people I saw were not creepy, unkempt, or intimidating. They weren't snarling or obviously maladjusted. Indeed, they were shocking in their ordinariness. This was a collection of the same men I've see in elevators, doctors' offices, restaurants, and the DMV—regular guys from work or your Facebook friend list. They were polite, well-dressed, and occasionally handsome. They looked like fathers, grandfathers, and stepfathers; coaches, teachers, and religious leaders—men from all different fields of work—because they were. Though that first group, and the many other predators I would meet in the coming years had committed sexual crimes against countless children, there was nothing immediately remarkable about them.

So if you are wondering whether there are any sexual predators in your children's orbit, I can spare you the uncertainty and confirm that yes, there are sex offenders or would-be sex offenders in your community. They are not necessarily on any registry. They have no background of known sexual crimes. They participate in groups where you are a member, and they live near you. You have met them already, and you do not know that they are predators. The good news is that you don't need to know who they are to protect your child.

There is no tidy demographic that alerts us to the presence of a likely predator—any adult or peer might turn out to be a sex offender. What we do know is that they are overwhelmingly adult and male (88 percent, according to victim-self report and law enforcement data[ii]). But a child's peers can also commit sex abuse, as can females, and this book details the risk factors and grooming strategies unique to those groups.

There also is no one place where abuse happens. Most often, it occurs in the child's home or the abuser's home, but predators are opportunists: Abuse occurs in schools and offices; on vacations and club trips; over mobile devices and school computers; through social media, online games, and private messaging—anywhere adults and children cross paths.

You may be wondering why I tell you not to panic or feel paranoid, if predators are indeed drawn to any environment where there are children. If we accept the reality that sexual predators are in our midst, we can deal forthrightly with the threat and set protective norms in place, thus significantly reducing the risks. Instead of drowning in denial or being paralyzed with fear, we can learn to recognize grooming and to be on the lookout for these signaling behaviors so that we are always prepared to protect a child.

Caring Adults Outnumber Predators

Before my work counseling child sex abusers, I assumed that most adults have no intention of harming the children they meet. This is still true: Your child is safe with most people, including those who work in settings like schools, hobbies, sports, and community activities. Adults who are drawn to work with children are most often excellent and caring people who wish to improve kids' lives. Remembering that will help you proceed calmly in enacting the recommendations in this book. Not only are most people not dangerous, but safe adults are essential to helping you keep your children safe. You can enlist them in setting up fail-safe protections for the children in your community.

The Child is What Matters

Since the spirit moved me to write this book I've mentioned it more than a few times in conversations. One thing I've learned from the people who don't run away at the topic (grittier than they were looking for at a backyard pool party!) is that people are fascinated by sex offenders. Daily, the news offers up fresh allegations of sexual crimes committed against children, complete with salacious descriptions. We read and watch these stories with insatiable appetites—we want to know what happened, lurid details and all. We especially want to find out about the perpetrators.

What Drives Our Fascination with Child Abusers?

We believe that knowledge is the key to keeping ourselves and our children safe, so we instinctively gravitate toward finding out what makes abusers tick—what made them who they are, and how do they think? We vaguely imagine that if we learn how predators wound up that way, we will be better able to prevent their actions from invading our own lives—as if intellectually understanding sexual predators will somehow shield our family from being the next victims.

Yet the factors contributing to the formation of a sexual predator are complex, individualized, and nonlinear. Even if they were clearer, in a magic formula that laid it out —"Here's what makes someone a sex abuser"— you would probably never know that a person had those damaging life experiences or carried those risk factors until they had already committed a crime against someone you know. Current treatment literature looks past popular myths about the formative influences on child abusers and sheds light on the influence of trauma, parenting, domestic violence, substance abuse, and biopsychosocial factors. (Refer to the Appendix for links to the latest research.)

But learning about sex offenders' drive for abusing will not help you protect the children around you. If anything, the constant stories of abuse dull our rightful sense of outrage at the horror of what is happening to many children.

We may also be scanning these tragic stories for reassurances of how we could never end up in the same situation. We look for how our relationships are all utterly different from the victims', how there is no one in our own circle who looks or sounds like the abuser on the news. But there are no ready-made markers or demographics that will clue you in to the presence of a predator. So, these self-assurances are false and empty.

How, Not Why

Your desire for knowledge is on track, but expending effort trying to understand why predators commit abuse misdirects your attention and wastes energy better spent on learning what actually will protect your family: How abusers groom their victims. That is what I felt compelled to share, because that is the knowledge that will keep your family safe.

Stop wasting time trying to understand child molesters or see the world as they do. Turn the tables. Instead of living in fear, wondering who might be scoping out your children, get ahead of the predators' game and begin to watch keenly for the potential sex offenders in your midst. This book offers you the active and practical task of becoming a watcher, one who calmly tracks the adults and peers in your child's life, so that you will have a better chance of discerning who might be a predator looking for prey.

Confident Champions for Children

Over the same years since I felt the call to write this book, I have also become the mother of five children. I understand, very personally, how much it means to feel confident that you know how to protect your beloved child from abuse. We all want our children to grow up safe from predators, to have the chance to be children while they still are.

Though its topic can be grim, this book is not a grueling voyage into the grisly details of child sexual abuse. Instead, it teaches you how potential predators groom, what grooming looks like in the spaces and situations children frequent, and how to reduce the risk of abuse for your child and other children.

You will learn how predators seek to gain access to your family and to create a bond of trust with you, all for their sexual benefit. As a fellow parent, I will teach you what to look for in adult behavior that may signify predatory tendencies, how to defend your children's innocence, and how to communicate effectively and clearly to keep children safer.

Prepared to Protect, Not Paranoid

When we assume that there are sexual predators in our schools and our communities and openly share that assumption, we all behave differently as attentive adults. Rather than acting out of fear, panic, and uncertainty, we can employ calm, clear-eyed determination and enact best practices for risk reduction. We spend time being open-eyed parents and active community members. We watch all adults with all kids, not just our own. We learn to be wary of adults who wish to be alone with children or behave as if the children were their peers. When we are paying close attention to adult behaviors, instead of drowning in paralyzing fear, we may notice something that can protect a child.

If I succeed in my mission—clearly spelling out the steps of grooming and giving you the courage to intervene—then perhaps one child will be safer and may never become the target of any predators in their midst. If we can spread this information to as many other parents and caring adults as possible, we can create a culture that leaves no prey available for child sex abusers anywhere.

INTRODUCTION

GROOMING 101 : PREDATORS AND PREY

The goal for all caring adults is for children to have the full opportunity to be children. We want them to be safe and cared for so that they will have plenty of chances to learn, grow, and explore their world. The adults who come in contact with children should be nurturing their growth and providing age-appropriate ways for them to follow their curiosity, to enjoy their young life, and to expand their capabilities.

Adults who take advantage of children's naïveté and relative powerlessness take away that opportunity. And since the overwhelming majority of child sex abusers are known and trusted by the abused child, these offenders also destroy the child's sense of basic safety and damage their ability to trust in others—usually with lifelong repercussions to the child's physical and mental well-being.

You can be prepared to stop abuse from happening if you know what to look for. We'll start by getting clear on some basic facts and terms.

Predators, Prey, and Traps

"Predator" and "prey" are not terms I ever used when I was in a therapeutic setting dedicated to rehabilitating adults who offended against children. "Predator" conjured up a dragon-like figure with the strength to take a life at any moment. But I was working with ordinary men who were, if anything, rather weak and easily cowed.

We are all familiar with the labels "sex offender" and "child molester," but neither is quite adequate for our focus here. For one thing, both terms describe people who have already committed a sexual crime against a child—a point that arrives late in the grooming process. My fervent hope is that all the would-be sex offenders in your midst fail—that their predatory aims against children remain permanently unsatisfied.

But also, neither phrase adequately captures the dynamic at work when someone is trying to gain access to a child for abuse. Outside the context of sexual abuse, "offenses" can be mild, and "molesting" might be mere annoyance—incidental or accidental. As I learned during my work with abusers, the process leading up to abuse is neither incidental nor accidental. It requires intent and cunning.

A predator is someone who injures or exploits another for personal gain or profit, which describes child sex abusers perfectly. Their prey are children, who are more defenseless than even a vulnerable adult, since a child cannot yet perform basic actions that give adults autonomy, such as driving or making money, nor do they have the life experience to spot mistreatment. For child sex abusers, a successful assault is the ultimate win, usually eclipsing any other goal (except to not get caught) so that they can maintain their freedom and continue to abuse. Predators find and exploit every opportunity to access children within their reach. They calculate and recalculate every setting and situation: "How can I get closer to this family?" "How can I become valued by this parent?" "Will anyone notice my moves toward this child?"

So the term "predator" fits child sexual abusers well. They follow a systematic process of tracking and trapping their targets—vulnerable children. Following the predictable stages of grooming, sexual predators scope out easy marks, set and bait a trap, rig the trap, then snap the trap and work to keep it shut. But there's nothing dragon-like about these sneaky predators. Ultimately, they are arrogant cowards and bullies who pick on people nowhere near their own size.

What is Child Sexual Abuse?

According to the US Centers for Disease Control and Prevention (CDC), child sexual abuse is "any completed or attempted (noncompleted) **sexual act, sexual contact with, or exploitation** (ie, noncontact sexual interaction) of a child by a caregiver."[iii] Any sexual activity involving a child, whether direct physical contact or through virtual or electronic means, is child sexual abuse and is a crime. Not all sex abuse involves sexual organs or direct physical contact, and it includes a wide range of offenses, from photographing a nude child to having intercourse with a child. (There is a list of the most common kinds of child sexual abuse in Chapter 6.)

The legal "age of consent" is 16, 17, or 18[iv], depending upon the state of residence, meaning all sexual activity with someone below that age is criminal. (Some states have special rules for when the people involved are close in age, in which case the sexual contact still may be assault, but it is not assumed to be based solely on the victim's age.) The "statute" in the term "statutory rape" is this law establishing that sex with a person who meets the definition of being unable to consent—in this case a child—is rape, no matter the intentions of any of the individuals involved. Even if the child willingly allows an abuser to engage in sexual contact with them—as predators will usually try to persuade their victims to do so that the child feels guilty and is more likely to stay quiet—the law says there is no such thing as consent from a child. Such cooperation is, by definition, coerced.

For the purposes of preventing child sex abuse, I encourage you not to get too caught up in the technicalities of what counts as illegal. Focus instead on what you know and believe to be wrong. The important takeaway from states' "age of consent" is that we share a broad societal consensus that using children and youth for sex is always wrong. Oddly, there's a persistent tendency to dance around this fact. Individuals and mass media sexualize minors and send problematic messages that contradict the civil consensus to protect children from being treated as sex objects. So this bears repeating: We all have to commit to the basic principle that children and youth are never used for sex.

Age of consent laws mark the lowest bar for some of the worst types of sex abuse: What someone can be arrested for. But I want to protect children, including teenagers[ii], from all forms of sex abuse—not just what's technically illegal. There are plenty of scenarios in which adults may not be breaking the law but are in the territory of abuse. Anyone who in a position of authority or control, using a child sexually in any way, we want to stop them before they start. We want to protect their victims—and that includes 17-year-olds in a state where the age of consent is 16, or 18-year-olds being manipulated into sexual relationships by predatory teachers or coaches.

With our words and our actions, we need to communicate to each other, to the children we are protecting, and especially to the predators in our midst that all children are off-limits to sexual predation. Although children of all ages are sensual beings who may be curious about sex, pleasure, and their bodies, it is always "closed season" for children and youth as sexual prey. They need time for maturation and to find love, trust, equality in partnership, a balance of desire, and a clear sense of their own sexual values before they are ready to be physically intimate with a partner—in their late adolescence at the earliest, and in early adulthood for most. Sexualizing children causes trauma and impedes their natural growth into healthy sexual beings. And it does not suddenly become "open season" on teenagers when they pass the legal age of consent; they continue to deserve our protection and watchful eye.

Who Commits Child Sex Abuse?

Any adult or peer can be a perpetrator of abuse. As I described earlier, they do not wear signs or have special tattoos. But since my framework for helping you prevent child sex abuse is risk reduction, it is useful for you to know the data about who poses the greatest threat.

As I learned in my work with sex offenders, and as statistics confirm above, most abusers are adults and most are male. Child-on-child sexual abuse, alarmingly, is on the rise (40 percent of all reported child sexual abuse allegations are peer-on-peer abuse[v]), and a small fraction of sex abusers are female. Throughout the book I use the "singular they" to refer to people when we don't know their gender. But when I need a singular pronoun in writing about a predator (outside the sections on female sex abusers), I will default to "he" based on the evidence that most child sex abusers are male.

Otherwise, there is no identifiable profile that predicts abuse. Predators hold every kind of role and title in communities, employment, and families. Fathers, grandfathers, neighbors, professionals, teachers, boyfriends, physicians, tutors, religious leaders, day care workers—the list goes on. No race, socioeconomic class, or professional industry lacks for abusive adults. People hear this fact, but they rarely let it sink in. It may be tough to believe or hard to remember, but the guy with the great suit, lovely car, and picture-perfect family can be an offender, too, not just the frayed person who makes you feel uncomfortable.

Because parents do not generally let their children hang out with complete strangers, a sexual predator usually has to know their prey to get close enough to be able to abuse them, or to begin grooming them for abuse. So the overwhelming majority of sex abusers—93 percent—are known to a child at the time of assault. About one third of these abusers (34 percent) are family members, and most of the rest (59 percent) are family acquaintances.[vi]

The scenario many parents fear most, of a stranger sexually assaulting their child, is less common, comprising 7 percent[vii] of perpetrators.

How Many Predators are There?

There are two main categories of known offenders. Pedophiles are individuals whose sexual desire for children develops in early adolescence, according to the Diagnostic and Statistical Manual of Mental Disorders, Fifth Edition. In the United States, an estimated 3 percent to 5 percent of adult males and 4 percent of adult females meet the criteria for a pedophile.[viii] It is impossible to estimate what percentage of pedophiles act on their desires.

According to the Rape, Abuse & Incest National Network (RAINN), only 31 of every 100 cases of child sexual abuse are brought to the police for investigation.[ix] Among those, just a fraction result in prosecution. Because sex abuse so often goes underreported, and not all predators are successful in abusing, we cannot know for sure what percentage of people are sexual predators who are looking for opportunities to abuse.

But many sexual offenders do not fit the criteria for pedophilia. They are adult males and females who tend to offend at later ages, often when life stressors, relationship difficulties, and intoxication from alcohol or other drugs disastrously combine with access to children. Research has yet to establish the percentage of non-pedophiles capable of sexually abusing children, in addition to the 4 percent to 5 percent of the general adult population who are pedophiles. Precisely because it is impossible to know how many predators there are, we all need to be aware and vigilant about protecting children.

Where Does Grooming and Abuse Happen?

Sexual predators corner their prey anywhere they can—homes, schools, churches, locker rooms, offices. This includes virtual spaces, through mobile phones, computers at school or home, in online games, and on social media platforms.

For risk reduction, you should know that most child sexual abuse occurs in the home of the child or the home of the predator (83 percent of all reported child sexual abuse, according to Darkness to Light data from 2012). Knowing that home can be a high-risk environment can help parents make practical and logical decisions to minimize that risk for their family. For example, as you assess your child's new friendship, you may rethink an indoor playdate and plan a park meetup instead, because research tells us there is lower risk of sexual abuse outside the home.

Grooming is easiest for a predator to accomplish in those same unseen spaces, but since much of grooming is simply conversation, it can happen almost anywhere. Anywhere adults or predatory peers come together with children, an aspiring abuser can begin pursuit. In rooms or outdoor spaces where people can be plainly seen but not overheard—including when a child is online and in view but their computer screen is not—a would-be sex offender can groom. And some grooming happens not only within sight but within the hearing of others who could intervene. Those others sadly lack either the understanding of grooming or the courage to step in. By the time you finish this book, neither of those descriptions will apply to you.

Who Are the Most Frequent Victims of Child Sex Abuse?

Any child can become the target of a sexual predator. To understand which groups are at highest risk, consider the data reporting which children predators target most often. By gender, 82 percent of victims are female. By age, 34 percent of victims are under the age of 12. The largest group of victims, 66 percent, are between 12 and 17 years old.[x]

According to the research, one in ten children in America[xi] will be sexually abused during childhood. Sadly, 60 percent of child sex abuse victims never tell anyone that it happened,[xii] bearing the trauma alone, in silence, and, too often, with misplaced guilt.

What Type of Child Is Most at Risk?

The question parents ask me most often is whether a predator selects a particular child or picks one randomly. My best answer is that sex abusers select the easiest available target. Predators constantly assess their environment for prey. They watch everything, observing children and what protections exist around each one. A child with the fewest protections is the one a would-be abuser tries to groom. Some vulnerabilities are internal—such as unmet needs in a child—and many are external: parental separation, domestic violence, financial instability, or absent protective structures in the child's family environment and community.

What Is Grooming?

Grooming for sex abuse is the methodical, predictable series of steps a predator takes toward a family and a child to gain their trust. If predators succeed, they gain access to the child, whom they then use for their own sexual exploitation.

Grooming is predatory. It includes hunting, hiding, stalking, and entrapment. Just as a poacher who is on land where they don't belong, sexual predators look for vulnerable or unprotected animals and lure them into traps.

Friendliness Isn't Grooming

Grooming is not any friendly behavior by an adult toward a child. Remember, caring adults outnumber predators. Also, sex abusers don't try to groom every child and family they meet. Grooming is not accidental, and it's not inevitable. But since it is also not random, and since child sex abuse is rarely a lightning bolt out of nowhere, you can prevent it or stop it once it starts.

The Relationship Is the Trap

What predators rely upon most to gain victims for abuse is a caregiver's belief that the predator is harmless and trustworthy—in fact, a uniquely wonderful person—rather than the would-be sex abuser that they are. Families become convinced that the predator is a true friend to the family and to the child. When the predators have accomplished their goal of sex abuse, they then rely on the trust they crafted with the family and with the community to manipulate and intimidate the child into silence—and to discredit the child's story if they do tell. They may also trade upon that trust to persuade the family not to press charges—and community members not to ostracize the abuser—even when the family does believe their child has been victimized.

The relationship—or, more accurately, the illusion of a wonderful relationship—is how sex abusers lure families and children into their trap. Sexual predators pretend to care about children and their families. They appear vulnerable, charming, and generous. But they are actors with one motivation that surpasses all others: to convince you to trust them with your child. Though their goal is hidden to most of us, it can become obvious when we pay closer attention.

Perverting the Strategies of Courtship

Dating is for peers and equals, but predators borrow pieces of the courtship ritual to suit their nefarious ends—time together, compliments, gifts, treats, telling their target how special they are. As creepy as it is for a sex abuser to treat their prey as if they were partners to be wooed, the dynamic, from the predator's perspective, is partly the same. They take extensive advantage of the child's gullibility as it suits them, but they also treat the child as an adult and equal if that helps them gain more access or deflects from their own guilt and failures.

Meanwhile, predators are also trying to earn your trust—just like someone who wants to impress a potential partner's friends and family. (In some cases, a would-be sex abuser even seeks a romantic relationship with a parent or guardian to obtain access to the children). But in all grooming, the abuser's ultimate target is a minor. So there is always a pernicious and intentional imbalance of power between the predator and the prey. A predator's undetected dishonesty gives them an unfair advantage; they know something you don't know—that they are sexually interested in your child and that their friendship is a ruse.

Predators Target the Family, Not Just the Child

The adults who seek out children for sexual pleasure and power trips do not want to tangle with strong, safety-savvy families. They consciously seek out families with fewer protections, more distractions, and greater instability: ideal prey. If they succeed in abusing a child, the victim will bear the heaviest toll of the trauma, but the whole family will be affected—or even destroyed. Thus, the stakes for prevention are high.

If your life is already difficult, especially for reasons beyond your control, it may feel unfair that you and your child are at increased risk of being targeted by a sexual predator. But the reality is that you are. My hope is that what you learn in these pages will make it easier for you to put the necessary guardrails in place to protect your family and to convince your community to help you enact those protections, and that it will persuade you of the importance of making that effort. When you have difficult decisions to make, and none of the options are great, the information in this book can guide you toward choices that reduce risk for your child.

It's on Us, the Adults

Prey are, by definition, those who are "helpless or unable to resist attack." Prey lack awareness of potential risks and threats, and as children are unaware of the full potential nefariousness of some adults or of dangerous peers, they are inherently unable to defend themselves. As you assess the possibility of child abuse, I hope you now understand that, in the wrong circumstances, any child might become prey to a sex abuser.

Some approaches to preventing child sex abuse focus primarily on teaching the child to spot and talk about possible grooming behaviors. It is absolutely necessary to teach a child awareness for their own safety. It also is true that the main way children can protect themselves is by communicating to a trusted adult immediately about their interactions with others—especially if they sense that something is amiss. A child should be told that they are never culpable for any abuse.

But even if they are brave and comfortable enough to share such information, it may be too late—after grooming attempts have already begun and perhaps progressed. If the predator is skilled at grooming, the child may not recognize that anything is amiss, ever—or not until long after the child is ensnared in the trap of abuse, ashamed, and afraid. For many reasons, it is not feasible to describe every potential scenario of grooming to children. So the primary responsibility to protect them lies squarely with the adults in their lives.

Stop here and take a moment to feel the full weight of our obligation. Since children are unaware of predators, it is our job to protect them. Children and teenagers cannot do this themselves, and it is not their fault if abuse happens. We must rigorously oversee their interactions with others and act as a force field around the children in our lives.

As adults, we can learn to realize when we are vulnerable, when we may be a target for predators, and when someone's behavior toward us or our child is concerning. Armed with the knowledge in this book, we can each refuse to let our families become prey. Indeed, we must.

CHAPTER 2

STOP GROOMING BEFORE IT BEGINS

As you learned in the last chapter, grooming is the process of pursuing a specific family and child to access the child for sexual contact. Every action is meant to gradually build trust with adults and gain access to children. Grooming is, therefore, a hundred or more tiny, opportunistic decisions and moves. Predators follow these predictable patterns once they find a family to groom. Your first step, which should be repeated for as long as you have children in your care, is prevention: Avoid becoming a targeted family. Within any family and community, it is the well-prepared adults who prevent child sexual abuse.

Your first instinct may be to give everyone who interacts with your children the benefit of the doubt, even if you feel a little uneasy or notice situations that create the opportunity for abuse. Predators take full advantage of that desire not to make waves. They rely on our ability to talk ourselves out of suspicions. How else would predators move within and among communities, leaving destruction in their wake? Turn this impulse on its head, and train your instinct towards calm, unapologetic vigilance.

Before Grooming Can Start

When a child's daily life puts them in regular contact with anyone, you have a responsibility as a parent, guardian, or caregiver to prevent the start of the grooming process. I hope you have come to this book in advance of any problem arising, so that you can put these important tools to use from the beginning of any relationship. But if you are here because something has already happened, or because you fear that your child may have been groomed or abused, know that the strategies in this stage also apply at every subsequent phase. You can always pay attention, listen to your gut, and learn to be assertive when it comes to protecting your child.

The stage when you are getting to know someone new is crucial. As is the time when you and your family are becoming closer with someone you already know, such as a cousin or family friend. The approach is the same. Your choices and communication set the terms of the relationship with anyone who may eventually spend time with your child. You want to make sure every person knows that the relationship is going to be on your terms—under conditions that ensure your child's safety.

Throughout this book I mostly refer to adults as the predators, as they commit the majority of sex offenses. But children do also sexually abuse other children. So notice anyone, of any age, who is hanging around your child. Apply the same prevention strategies to peers and older children as you apply to adults, whenever the strategy is applicable.

And always remember: Most people are not sexual predators, but the ones who are stay busy scanning for fresh prey. From the first meeting, a predator constantly assesses every opportunity for grooming in any place your family or child frequents—including school, special events, clubs, church or religious communities, sports leagues, peer groups, and digital spaces. That initial get-to-know-you stage is your first chance to make sure that sex abusers move along without ever harming your child, your family, or your community.

Your prevention strategies at this stage are simple, though they may take some practice:

PAY ATTENTION

When anyone is spending time with or near your child, get to know them and be observant. Notice what they talk about and how they look at your child and other children. Be present at events if you can, or have a trusted substitute—like a grandparent or an attentive, assertive babysitter— observe and fill you in. Every predator keenly recognizes the kids with spotty supervision, disgruntled relationships with primary caregivers, or empty spaces in their lives—figurative and literal. Note, too, how the physical or electronic spaces are configured where this person and your child will be interacting, what other adults and children are present, and what the plans are for communicating with your family. I recommend that through at least age 15, all communication about a child's plans or activities include or go directly to the adult caregiver, with no notes or electronic messages sent privately from an adult to a child. Notice whether anyone is resistant to having you around or seems to be trying to get rid of you.

Paying attention in this manner is preventive, not paranoid. Even if someone is a predator, their first interactions with children and their parents are usually no different from those with the many safe non-predators among us.

An aspiring sex offender may be welcoming, outgoing, and friendly to you and your family—they want to blend in. As time goes on, the first observable sign may actually be this attention. Before any real grooming begins, a would-be sex abuser might pay just a little more attention to your child than to other children, or lavish more attention than most people usually give you, your child, and your family. Notice. You are being tested to see if you are a good target.

START STRONG

When you and your child are meeting someone, introduce yourself assertively. Use ordinary small talk. Establish yourself as an interested, engaged, aware adult. For example, approach anyone working near your child and introduce yourself at the first available occasion. Confidently make eye contact, firmly extend your hand to shake theirs, and make conversation. Ask what brings them to your community, where they were before, and how they came to this volunteer role or job. "How did you decide to join our church?" "Have you been a scout leader before?" "What else do you do, for fun or work?" "What do you enjoy about working with fifth graders?" Your tone is light and friendly. This is not an interrogation, and it is not a date. Your posture, tone, and confidence show the person joining your world that you are interested in them because they are going to be affecting your family. If you typically act reserved, asserting yourself in these interactions may take some practice, but it is vital for your children's safety that you learn.

NOTICE OTHER PEOPLE'S BEHAVIOR TOO

In addition to staying aware of a person's interactions with your child, notice how they act with other staff and co-workers. Is there anything that makes you take a second look? How do others react to them? (You may not notice anything out of the ordinary, because there may be nothing unusual to notice.)

ADDRESS UNEXPLAINABLE UNEASE

Your best early-warning system that someone might be a potential threat is your own gut—a sense of vague skepticism or unease is often the first sign of a problem. Take the time to notice your inner responses, even if you cannot quite explain them. In *The Gift of Fear,*[xiii] safety expert Gavin de Becker discusses how we are all hardwired with strong instincts to keep ourselves and our children safe and how, unfortunately, we often override those reactions. We talk ourselves out of listening to our gut with reasons such as concern about how others will judge us or think we're being mean or unfair. Stop it. Assertively evaluate your gut response to a situation, and pull back from that situation if you're concerned. Change the setup, and be willing to change the team, the plan, or the overall arrangement if something is not sitting well with you. You choose how your child spends their time.

NOTICE YOUR CHILD'S RESPONSE

If your child has a strong reaction to a person in their life, positive or negative, make note of it. There are plenty of good reasons for a child to be excited about a new activity. They may feel happy about the promise of mentorship from an adult or just enjoy being with an older child they are getting to know. But an outsized amount of excitement should be just as alarming as distress. Recognize the child's body language around the person, and notice the way your child speaks about them.

STAY STEADY AND UNAPOLOGETIC

Beyond the first introduction, stay engaged and attentive. Predators are patient—they have to be, to get what they want. So be diligent. Continue to make conversation, continue to observe behavior directly, and continue to notice your own gut and your child's reactions. From first contact forward, through the duration of each relationship, show that your child, your family, and your community are paying close attention. Make it clear that this is not a community that will let itself fall victim to a predator.

The Predictable Stages of Grooming

An overview of the whole grooming process will give you a sense of what we're trying to prevent. Here are the four stages of unimpeded grooming: 1) Setting the Trap 2) Baiting the Trap, 3) Rigging the Trap with Guilt, and 4) Keeping the Trap Snapped Shut. The favored tools for the stages move from compliments to favors, then separating children from their protectors, and finally threats and manipulation.

FIRST STAGE: SETTING THE TRAP WITH COMPLIMENTS

Having found a promising target, a predator begins to Set the Trap. The trap is the relationship—the fake bond that the predator will act out to gain access to your child. In this first stage of grooming, the main tool the would-be sex abuser uses is compliments—positive attention toward the family and the child. Hoping to create a bond of trust, the predator wants the family to think highly of him and to believe that he admires and cares for them.

If the predator's early efforts succeed, the family is enthusiastically supporting this budding relationship: They think this new person is wonderful. This high regard early on sets up a misplaced trust in this adult (or peer) who is entering the child's life. The differences between grooming and a nice new friendship can be difficult to spot if you don't know what you're looking for. I want you to be prepared.

As a caring adult seeking to block all efforts at grooming—including the earliest and most subtle—the key to risk reduction is having sturdy protocols for managing access to your child. Then, even if a new relationship doesn't show any clear signs of inappropriate behavior, it will be easier to block opportunities for predation later.

SECOND STAGE: BAITING THE TRAP WITH FAVORS

If the relationship is the trap, the bait for the trap is favors, because being super-helpful makes a friendship harder to resist or walk away from. Once a predator believes he has earned some level of trust from the adult gatekeepers, he will start to help the child or the family. Offers may include free babysitting, extra time with the predator (whom the child and family enjoy), or gifts. Families in need of financial or emotional support are at extra risk of a predator's deceiving kindness. In the Baiting the Trap stage, a child is also likely to start receiving the predator's direct, personalized attention, including intangible and perhaps tangible gifts.

If grooming is succeeding at this stage, the potential sex abuser seems kind and loving to your child and like a unique blessing and support to your family, and you feel completely comfortable having them in your life and your child's. It is a deceivingly sweet spot in the relationship with the predator, if you haven't caught on to their act.

The challenge in this stage of grooming is that it's hard for adults to push back against the seeming wonderfulness of the relationship. But if grooming has made it this far, you are at a crucial tipping point because the leap to the next stage is a long one into much darker territory. If you fail to stop it now, it will be harder to detect and intervene in the next stage—and families that accept a predator's bait will move unwittingly and rapidly toward abuse. Fortunately, though, a sexual predator baiting his trap supplies transparent clues for the adult whose eyes are open. (More on those in Chapter 4.)

THIRD STAGE: RIGGING THE TRAP WITH GUILT

If the family's trusting relationship with the predator is the trap that makes abuse possible, the child's relationships with safe adults are the only reliable escape routes. The abuser now intentionally and subtly separates the child from their protective adults, physically and emotionally. After the success of the first and second stages, parents and other protectors already trust this helpful, charming person. The adult barrier has been nudged aside, and the predator homes in directly on the child.

What this stage looks like is a special relationship emerging between the predatory adult and the preyed-upon child. The predator has two angles to separating the child from protectors, one resembling the favors of the previous stage, the other taking a bleaker turn. Usually, this stage is still more carrot than stick, with predators luring children with additional bait—things like mental games, secret bonds, and unique experiences. But the would-be sex abuser may also start emotionally manipulating the child—making the child feel guilty for not going along with the abuser's plans, or perhaps ashamed of some of those secret experiences.

If grooming has progressed to this stage, it is absolutely crucial that caring adults detect it and intervene to halt the progression toward abuse. If a predator succeeds in this stage, abuse is inevitable. The child will see no escape routes, no path other than to stay trapped in abuse.

The main challenge at this point for caring adults is combatting the predator's efforts to tempt a child away from their protective relationships. Children do not understand when they are in danger of being exploited, especially by someone who is likeable and perhaps popular. And a determined sex abuser can be cunning, stealing time for the special bonding with the child and for the darker emotional manipulations, all outside the parents' awareness. He is also working to persuade the child not to talk about their secret bonds to test whether they will report questionable behaviors. At this point, effective intervention to stop abuse will require a parent to peel back the trust the family has developed in this adult.

Fortunately, grooming scenarios in this stage can be discernible to an attentive, well-informed adult. While the specific grooming behaviors may take place out of sight, the amount of time spent with the predator can be a big red flag. Even someone who doesn't know what to look for might think, "Those two are unusually close—something is making me a little curious here." During this critical stage, safe adults can offer a lifeline to the child, re-introducing whatever protections the child needs while going on the offense to drive the predator away.

FOURTH STAGE: KEEPING THE TRAP SNAPPED SHUT

The turning point to this fourth and final phase is that sexual abuse begins. The predator snaps the trap to fulfill his primary ends: using the child for physical pleasure, sexual dominance, or both.

It seems like at this stage, the grooming would be considered to be over. But the predator has not yet fulfilled all his goals, and continued grooming is essential to his ultimate success. Part of the perpetrators' mission is to not get reported for his crimes or face any consequences. Furthermore, most sex offenders continue their abuse, often with the same child and with others. According to statistics, 70 percent of sex offenders have one to nine victims, and an additional 20 percent of sex abusers have 10 to 40 victims.[xiv] These are persistent, serial criminals. They need to maintain their act—the illusion that they are trustworthy—if they are to maintain their access to children. So even after an assault, the abuser keeps grooming—to ensure silence and further ongoing victimization—to avoid detection and keep the trap shut with his prey inside.

To the inattentive observer, this stage may look similar to the previous one, when the predator and the prey simply have a special relationship. But the abuse stage has its own signs, which you can learn to spot.

Sadly, if a sexual predator has abused a child, all of the available adults have looked the other way more than once—staying silent and either ignoring or failing to recognize the predation patterns that allowed the child to fall into the trap. Protectors' ineffectiveness has likely confirmed the victim's fear that there is nowhere to turn. So now, more than ever, it is those adults' responsibility to spot the abuse and step in to end it. It may be too late to prevent the first abuse, but it is never too late to free the victim from the trap, protect them from further abuse, and start them on the road to healing in mind and spirit.

What's Ahead

A would-be sex abuser works stealthily through the stages. Usually, each stage takes time, but not always. Online predators, for example, move rapidly through all the stages of grooming: Predation carried out online, on children whose caregivers allow them unmonitored internet access, may take mere days. And if a predator realizes he is losing ground with a family or a child, he may repeat a stage until he regains enough trust. The time needed for each stage differs, depending on how long it takes the predator to set up or reestablish trust.

Each of the next four chapters is dedicated to a grooming stage, with practical recommendations for how to prevent, identify, and intervene in any grooming attempts. These chapters also function as a handbook for how to address grooming that may have already begun. They will give you a "cheat sheet" for recognizing a predator's moves and for addressing and thwarting abuses in everyday life.

Then Chapters 7 through 12 focus on the common variations on the grooming template, specific to certain situations and roles others play in a child's life. Certain spaces (such as your home) and roles (such as doctors or coaches) afford a predator unique access opportunities that you need to be aware of in order to spot easily. This section helps you develop a preemptive plan for reducing opportunities for predators, wherever your child may encounter them.

Finally, I end with two chapters dedicated to building and reinforcing protections for individual families and communities, to guide you as you make decisions for your family. Let's get started.

UNDERSTANDING THE TRAP

CHAPTER 3

FIRST STAGE OF GROOMING : SETTING THE TRAP WITH COMPLIMENTS

Grooming starts when an eager predator chooses a family. Predators train their awareness on what a family craves, then appear to try to fill that need. They work to figure out what you want to hear, and then they will say anything that they think will get you to eventually hand over your child. If they set the trap convincingly and invisibly in this first stage of grooming, you will not only allow them to have a relationship with your child, you will encourage it.

Observable, Predictable Grooming Moves

A predator starts with you—the child's guardians and protectors. Since minor children are your responsibility and, in your care it is your trust that predators need if their plan is to progress. The child's trust will be easy enough to earn once they have cleared the adult hurdle. Their typical moves include special treatment and flattery about you and the child, fanning competition for their attention and making themselves seem fun or special to the child. All of this interaction allows them to identify the weak spots in your family—which may have been what drew the predator in the first place.

FLATTERY

Compliments are intoxicating. All of us are at risk of falling for a convincing ego stroke, and predators know it. They are motivated actors, highly skilled at building up you and your child. They compliment your parenting and discuss your wonderful, special son or daughter. Accolades for a child's performance in an activity may be well-earned, but they might also, or instead, be a predator's way to position themselves as your family's favorite coach or teacher.

TREATING YOUR CHILD AS EXCEPTIONAL

While making flattering remarks to the parent, a predator compliments the child too. Children naturally crave attention and recognition for their efforts. And all parents are eager to find caring adults who want to help their children improve their confidence and discover new pursuits. In this early stage of grooming, predators count on this basic human desire to thrive to "Set the Trap." If they emphasize or even fabricate stories about your child's uniqueness—which you earnestly believe in and wish for—predators can earn your trust quickly. An adult who lauds your child as special is likely to inspire your confidence.

COMPETITION AS A TOOL

In activities that offer limited opportunities for promotion, competition among children can be fierce. Predators often obtain positions of authority in such activities so they can exploit a family's willingness to encourage their child in that endeavor. And when a family believes that the adult holds the keys to a child's advancement, this person becomes indispensable to the family. There may even be competition for the predator's attention and favoritism as parents seek opportunity for their child. This competition among children for an adult's affection gives predators even greater influence: The more popular the predator becomes in a community, the more untouchable he becomes.

PREDATORS UNDERSTAND KIDS

Successful sex abusers are incredibly skilled at bonding with kids. They are typically outgoing and, most importantly, available—while other busy adults may not be. Predators go out of their way to connect with children. They may act more childlike, silly, and playful than other adults or, conversely, treat children as adult peers. They seem wonderfully giving of their time, but predators' goals are always selfish.

LIKEABILITY AND POSITIVE PUBLIC OPINION

You might assume that one of the clues to identifying a predator is that you dislike them and don't know why. But the opposite is true. The predators most likely to succeed in grooming children are the ones who seem compassionate, caring, vulnerable, harmless, charismatic, or generous.

More often, you will like them—maybe more than you like most people. As I noticed so vividly in my own work, sexual predators are not what you would imagine. They are not obviously creepy, sleazy, or threatening. They are usually people we enjoy, whom we encourage our children to spend time with, whom we speak of highly to our families and communities.

But how much you or your community appreciates, trusts, awards, and exalts a person is no measure of their risk to your family or your child. In fact, good character traits can blind us to a predator's progressive and escalating steps toward abuse. I cannot emphasize this point strongly enough: Not only is a person's likeability not an assurance that they are a safe adult, but it is often an essential dimension of a predator's entrapment strategy. A positive reputation makes us ignore potential danger, so building that reputation is part of the trap—part of the would-be sex abuser's strategy to gain access to children. The more people who think this person hung the moon, the fewer there will be to believe the truth if he gets caught sexually abusing kids.

In the previous chapter, I insisted that you do a gut-check to gauge whether someone makes you uneasy. But not everyone who makes us suspicious is someone we don't like. Just as often, we have a tough time admitting that we're uneasy about someone—precisely because we are also incredibly fond of them. That inner tension is the result of a predator trying hard to make sure you like him, trying to make sure you ignore your gut. The challenge we face as parents is to see through a predator's façade. If you find yourself liking someone more than is typical for you, that in itself is a signal that you need to watch this relationship carefully— whether or not that person makes you uneasy.

SCANNING FOR VULNERABILITIES

A predator chooses a family because he has sensed vulnerabilities to exploit. During the first stage of grooming, to set the trap, he targets those vulnerabilities and looks for additional weak spots. These could include difficulties in a marriage, financial instability, or a challenging child. A predator also looks for gaps in a child's and family's life that need to be filled. These gaps may be practical, such as transportation challenges, or more subtle, such as emotional needs. A would-be sex abuser shows particular interest in and understanding about difficulties in your life.

BUILDING A CONNECTION WITH THE CHILD

Predators become a warm and understanding resource for the child at this stage of grooming. If the early flattery works, they then supply an ear that the primary caregiver may not be able to give. Predators say things like "You can talk to me," "I am here for you," "I like spending time with you best," or "You are unlike any other child I've ever met"—continuing the tactics of flattery and reassurances of specialness. Perversely, this relationship building can have the feel and language of a courtship, as if the predator were wooing the child. So be on alert if you notice language that reminds you of peers dating. Don't pretend that language is cute between a child and an adult, and don't jokingly borrow language from dating to describe the relationship.

Conflicts between a child and their guardians will inevitably arise from time to time, and a predator will exploit them. (This behavior will escalate if grooming progresses to the next stage.) They may respond to the child's frustration with "You can talk to me if you need someone" or "I wouldn't treat you like your parents do." Predators are highly attuned to any dearth of acceptance in a child's life, whether from family, other adults, or peers. The child's struggle is, unfortunately, a predator's gain.

What to Notice in a Child

If a child is having age-appropriate experiences, many of them in child-centered environments, they will get to know lots of people. Forming and deepening relationships with adults and peers is one of the benefits of many childhood activities. And at this stage of grooming, even if a predator has started setting the trap with observable, flattery-based behaviors, there is probably little to see in the behavior of the child. But there may be a few clues, so here are a couple of dynamics to watch for in a child.

CHILDREN LIKE THE ADULT

While flattering you and cultivating your trust, a grooming predator is also seeking to form a friendship with your child. Not everyone who befriends your child is a predator, but friendship is an essential element of the grooming process, so be aware of whether your child is having a notable response to someone. The child may say things like "he's cool" or just "he's okay." Children want approval and attention. Any adult who shows your child attention, affection, and kindness can become important in their lives. Conversely, a child may not even notice the attention. As a parent, simply stay alert to your child's reactions.

THE CHILD COMPETES FOR SPECIAL ATTENTION

Competition among peers for privileges and promotions motivates most children. There is power in being the favorite scout, teacher's pet, or most valuable player. Children learn quickly to position themselves to receive accolades, and, for vulnerable children, a predator's attention can mean everything. Notice if your child is striving hard to be the best or most rewarded in a certain activity, and stay alert to who is leading that activity and whether they might be egging on that competition to be the top kid.

THE CHILD IGNORES OR DISLIKES THE PREDATOR

By having a negative or unenthusiastic reaction during the initial stages of grooming—or later—a child can knowingly or unknowingly deter a sex abuser. Predators change course depending on a child's response to their grooming efforts, and children who ignore or avoid grooming prompts demonstrate that they aren't good prey.

But if a child likes a person enthusiastically and is taken in by a grooming process, they have in no way aided or encouraged their abuser. It is never the child's fault that they have been groomed or abused. Ever. Predators always seek out young, unprotected prey, and it is adults' work to prevent and intervene in any predation. Baby animals can never adequately defend themselves against attacks from dangerous stronger animals—that is the job of their parents, pack, and herd. So we can be thankful if a child somehow deters the process of grooming, but it is never their fault if they don't. That's on us.

Practical Recommendations for Caring Adults

Maintain all the preventions you learned to practice before any grooming starts: pay close attention, be present and assertive, and note your own inner reactions. And if you suspect that you may be seeing some first efforts at grooming—some set the trap behaviors—here are interventions to enact with yourself and others.

REPLACE VANITY WITH VIGILANCE

If any relationship that involves your child is unusually heavy in compliments, become more vigilant. The same rule applies to someone who isn't spending time with your children yet but might in the near future—such as a new boyfriend. Do not fall for the flattery about yourself, your family, or your child. If an adult or older child seems head over heels for your child, you need to watch that relationship closely.

USE YOUR PARENTAL SKEPTICISM

Anyone showing increased attention toward your child should inspire more of your attention and supervision. Always keep a realistic perspective about the adults working with your child. No matter what anyone may tell you, no person's opinion of your child is the be-all, end-all. If you feel enchanted with a new person who's working to build trust with your family, notice your reaction and increase your vigilance about the adult, rather than letting your guard down readily—which is a predator's intention.

BE WARY OF THE UNICORN

If your child is truly gifted and talented, then it is likely that doors will open and opportunities will multiply. A predator convinces families he is the "unicorn," the one person who can improve the child's opportunities. Be wary of people who say they are the only expert who can bring your child's dreams to fruition. Repeatedly, we see increased parental deference to a unicorn coach or instructor allowing predators to move easily from setting a trap to the next phase, Baiting the Trap. Abuse is too high a price to pay for a championship or award. Don't fall for the act.

REFRAIN FROM GUSHING

If you do like someone a lot, whether it's a coach or a teacher, a doctor or a new romantic partner, be circumspect in how you talk about them while you're still getting to know them. Resist the urge to praise them effusively, especially in front of your child, even though nothing bad has happened at this early stage. If, unbeknownst to you, this new adult is trying to groom your child, they are giving the child flattering attention, too, and making space for conversation, time together, and skill building. If your child then hears that you admire this adult, they are apt to adopt your views. Placing trust and confidence in your opinion, your child is encouraged to assume that this individual is worthy of their trust. Be measured and mindful of how you talk about the people in your child's life.

MAKE YOUR CHILD SPECIAL

You own the keys to making your child feel special. Speak to, listen to, and look at your child as a routine part of being an attentive parent. Don't assume that your child knows you love them: Have positive interactions to show your child you care. The strongest bond in your child's life needs to be with you. Any exceptional bond forming with your child and another adult is a warning sign for parents. Notice what gaps of love and attention may have developed in your child's life, and fill them.

The Takeaway

This early stage, preventing predators from setting the trap, asks you, as parents, to watch the adults approaching your family. Most adults aren't trying to abuse children, but there are predators in all settings. Open your eyes and ears wide: Is a sweet and caring figure set on learning more about you, your child, and your family? Is someone constantly telling you how wonderful you and your child are?

Guard your seat as the primary protector of your child and family. If you love your child and show them how lovable they are, there will be less space for a potential predator. Set yourself now as the force field of protection between your family and unknown predators. No adult, no matter their role, has a right to access your child.

CHAPTER 4

SECOND STAGE : BAITING THE TRAP WITH FAVORS

If a predator succeeds in setting the trap in the first stage of grooming, they have flattered you and convinced you that they are a blessing to your family. You feel lucky to have them around and glad for their attention, and you may hope that your relationship becomes closer. They may have attained a valuable role in your child's life already and, perhaps, an elevated status in your community. They have earned your trust. All the while, that predator is constantly reassessing the relationship, working hard to deepen that trust. In the next stage of grooming, Baiting the Trap, this nefarious actor starts finding any possible reason to be close to your family and your child. It's crucial to learn how to recognize efforts at laying bait—favors and gifts—and what to do in response.

Children don't always have words to express their experiences or the perspective to even recognize them as noteworthy, and sexual predators depend on a child's ignorance in their pursuit of abuse. But to others, the moves are clearer at this stage. When you step up to intervene and avert grooming now, you are not only preventing your child from being pursued by a possible predator, but you are teaching them how to handle favors and gifts more generally, with wisdom and awareness.

The wisdom of experience teaches us to move slowly enough in relationships to know whether we can trust a person before we share with them additional levels of our safety, privacy, tender feelings, or indebtedness. In a relationship that involves contact with your child, the imperative to move slowly applies tenfold.

Observable, Predictable Grooming Moves

The trap child sex abusers use to ensnare families is the relationship—the illusion of an open, honest friendship—and the most common bait to draw you further in and seal the bond is favors. If there is one word to describe a predator's behavior at this stage, it is *helpful*. Predatory adults are often generous with their time and talents: They volunteer, start foundations, and exhibit countless other kindnesses. If a predator has targeted your child for grooming, they now focus some of that deceptive selflessness directly on your family.

OFFERS TO HELP

In this baiting stage, a predator clearly wants to help you and your family, but it is only a manipulative means to the invisible end: abuse. A frequent tactic is offers to drive, babysit, or supervise your child. Most busy parents, possibly desperate for time to tend to adult tasks or to rest, welcome this help. Meanwhile, the predator is creating a role for themselves within your child's life and yours. They become a regular presence in day-to-day life that you, the whole family, and the child all take for granted. Their hope is to become indispensable, so that you need them and will be even more disposed to trust them and depend on them. Then the doors of full, solitary access to your child will be wide open.

CREATING ALONE TIME WITH YOUR CHILD

As a friend to your family, a predator starts seeking out tiny bits of time alone with your child. You see no evidence of harm, so you freely allow your child to be alone with this person. The would-be predator, a professional liar, is following a recipe for deepening trust: Your family is coming to depend on this adult, and you believe he is contributing positively to your child's life. If the predator's efforts to connect directly with your child are succeeding, the child may be enthusiastic about spending more time with this generous adult. All this combines to result in your child and the predator spending more and more time together, bit by bit by bit.

GIVING GIFTS, MONEY, AND PROMOTIONS

All child sexual abuse involves imbalances between predator and prey—in maturity, age, title, physical size, financial status, or position—and predators leverage their advantage. Because most child sex abusers are adults, they usually have glaringly more power in all these categories than the child they are preying upon, and the child usually overestimates that power even further. The predators then use whatever influence and capabilities they have as means of seeming generous to a child.
Gifts are a favorite method of influence. Seasoned predators know that gifts work to entice children and families. Gifts come in many forms, tangible and intangible. If possible, a predator uses money and items that cost money on his targeted prey. It may not take much money to seem like a lot to a child. So be on the lookout for gifts to your child, large or small. Physical items are the easiest to spot, including cash, food, presents, and mementos. Tickets to a show the child could not afford, money for clothes or new electronics, or an extravagant birthday present are common baits of a grooming predator. A new item in your child's room is noteworthy, especially if you don't know where it came from. If the item turns out to be a gift from an adult, pay attention.

A predator may also send gifts directly to you and your family, such as cash or equipment, or they may pay or waive enrollment fees or registration expenses for activities.

GIVING INTANGIBLE GIFTS

Favors don't cost money and don't have a physical presence, which can make them a little harder to spot. So stay alert. Children and youth want to advance in their activities, and parents sometimes want that success even more than the children do. Gifts, in this context, can include positions on a team or special roles in a group that give the child seniority among peers. Parents want to believe that all such upgrades are well-earned, but force yourself to evaluate whether your child is receiving special treatment for no discernible reason.

INCREASING TIME TOGETHER

In addition to giving physical objects, predators may facilitate a child's participation in shared activities that will maintain or increase their time together. That gift of tickets to a concert is likely to include the adult taking the child to the show. Bringing someone to a special private event is another type of gift that adds to time together. Invitations to come over for a meal, go out for a game, or go to a movie set the child apart from the rest of their peer group.

HAVING A TYPE

Predators often have a type, seeking certain features, a specific appearance, a physical build, or a personality type when looking for their ideal prey. They usually have a gender and age preference for who they select to groom for abuse. These preferences are observable to caring and watchful adults.

What to Notice in a Child

If a child is being groomed successfully, the most obvious pattern to look for is a positive reaction to the person who is working to get close to them. The child wants more of their attention and favors.

APPRECIATING THE ADULT OR OLDER PEER

A child is likely to view any adult in a favorable light if they give the child gifts and promotions—it's a natural reaction. They will perceive the predator as cool, kind, or caring. Indeed, some people are cool, kind, and caring—and most are not predators. But if you see that a child is having a strong reaction to an adult or older peer who is in a position of power over them, take note.

RECEIVING GIFTS AND RECOGNITION

Children love presents, especially if they come from an adult they care about, so it is easy to use gifts to lead them blindly into a trap. A child may have no concept of how someone might use gifts to make them feel indebted later, so it is up to you, as the adult, to spot inappropriate gifts or patterns of gift-giving, recognition, or promotion. A child's ignorance is always a predator's tool, so don't bring a childlike naivete to any gifts you or your child may receive.

REACTING NEGATIVELY

On the other hand, a child will occasionally respond negatively to an adult's attention. The child may not like being singled out, or they may have a vague sense that something is amiss. They may not, however, have the vocabulary or the social acumen to understand and articulate what's really bothering them. The child may express their discomfort indirectly—saying they no longer like the activity or something about a program.

If a predator is skilled, a negative reaction is unlikely at this stage—but it is possible. So if you see this response in your child, it is important. Remember that a child can sometimes thwart a predator before you even detect a hint of a problem. There are any number of innocuous reasons your child may not want to go to soccer practice. But if you notice a strong reluctance to be in a certain place or with certain people, always keep in mind that there could be a situation evolving that a child doesn't know how to describe or doesn't want to share. And never force your child to spend time alone with a person who makes them uneasy.

Practical Recommendations for Caring Adults

If a predator has groomed their way past the beginning of baiting his trap, you are now a member of his fan club. That gives the would-be child abuser the green light to move on to the next stage, which is a long leap toward abuse. Beware of that fan-club feeling. It is a blatant clue that something is amiss.

Parents are the authority on drawing and redrawing the expectations for their family. Don't cede that responsibility to anyone, and don't allow someone's apparent generosity to sway you from your values or principles. You are the architect of the force field of safety around your child.

BE HONEST WITH YOURSELF

Perform a fan-club gut check on yourself. If you, the caregiver, have been effectively and unwittingly groomed, you'll feel disappointed at the mere thought that this person could be a predator, and you may be reluctant to even consider the possibility. Do it anyway.

It's difficult at this stage, because you consider this person an asset to your family. You value their attention and help, and you welcome their encouragement of your child. Your child enjoys this person's company while participating in activities. You appreciate the rides home after practice, the volunteering to spend time with your child outside of scheduled practices, the encouragement to your child to arrive early to rehearsal, the easy, free-spirited play with your kids, the way their office is always open to your daughter or son.

If grooming has crept in unnoticed, these small amounts of alone time the predator orchestrates with your child seem like special opportunities, not dangers. You may hear yourself speaking highly of this person to your friends, in front of your child, and in your community. And the small gifts you were receiving early in this stage will have become bigger. By the end of the predator's baiting the trap, you are "munching" happily on their favors, not realizing the threat to your child and family.

DO NOT SING THE ADULT'S PRAISES YET

If your family is in this second stage of grooming, your child is still experiencing, parallel incentives: positive attention from this new person and enthusiasm about that person within the family. Keep squelching the urge to gush about how wonderful this person is and how lucky the child is that they have come into your lives.

COMMUNICATE DIRECTLY

As someone becomes closer to your family or more a part of your child's life, your role at this stage of possible grooming is to be direct, watchful, and curious. Actively communicate with your child, listening carefully, to learn about their experiences.

Also communicate clearly with this adult (or influential peer) to establish your family's expectations around any interactions with your child. Effective parenting requires you to talk, directly and assertively, to anyone who is a part of your child's life.

SHOW UP

Your main job is simple: observe. Become a fixture at your child's events or activities. If an adult has been flattering you or your child or showing them extra attention, watch even more closely. If you are unavailable, have someone else—a trusted family member or another adult—be present whenever your child has activities.

The best way to observe is to show up in person and watch during any times when parents are invited—such as games and performances—and when they are not. Be early for pick-up and listen or observe from a distance. Occasionally drop by unannounced: "I finished my meeting early and thought I'd come on up."

If you are not available, and neither is a stand-in, make sure that all events involving an adult and your child are in large groups. Better still, select activities with groups of children where more than one (unrelated) adult supervises.

KNOW AN ACTIVITY'S ADULT-CHILD PROTOCOLS

I will delve further into best child safety practices for groups in Chapter 14. For now, it is enough to say that if a program discourages parent observation or includes time when an adult leader is entirely insulated from the view of other adults, reconsider your child's participation—even if you have already begun the activity. If you realize an organization lacks strong protocols to keep children safe, look for another venue or program that supports parental supervision.

Adults who give individual lessons to children and youth, and any adults who hang out with children, should stay where other adults, children, and parents are around and where they can be easily observed or overheard. To prevent opportunities for grooming, avoid putting your child in isolated one-on-one settings.

SAY NO TO THE "NEVER QUIT" MINDSET

Parents who enforce a "never quit the team" policy set up a tricky situation when a predator is involved. Parents want their children to learn commitment and to honor their obligations, but the "never quit" mantra makes it easier for a predatory adult or peer to harass the child—trapping them regularly in the presence of their harasser.

When a child says negative things about an adult or a team experience, such parent's adherence to the policy can supersede consideration for the child's well-being; this is a gift for a predator. If you disregard a child's perspective and discontentment, you allow an abuser to manipulate the child into believing that no one cares about them. Except, of course, for the predator.

Be a family where taking part in an activity brings happiness, not misery. If you have a suddenly unhappy child in a hobby or sport, for no discernible or fixable reason, remove your child and move on to the next experience. Children feel helpless when they face judgment from their families about quitting a negative experience with a creepy adult or peer. If your child approaches you about quitting, offer them the choice to switch to a new team, coach, or facility. The root of the problem may be the adults or peers tied to that location.

REFUSE SPECIAL GIFTS, AS A FAMILY POLICY

This recommendation goes to the heart of intervention at this stage: You must be ready to refuse gifts, even when you don't want to. If the giver is an unknown predator, the gifts are designed to hit you where you need them most—so personalized and wonderful that it can be hard to say no. Already, you may not think twice about your child spending time with this adult, and if you accept generosity, too, you add a sense of indebtedness —a feeling in yourself and perhaps in your child that you owe this person something. That is the predator's plan. Human nature and basic social expectations assume some kind of reciprocity when people are nice to us, especially when they go out of their way or exceed routine niceties. Accepting personal, unique favors indicates that the receiver feels a level of trust and safety with the giver. Welcoming someone's time, attention, and gifts sends the message that you believe them to be friend, not a threat. Predators know that if you accept their generosity, you will feel some obligation to them—even if they insist that you needn't or you tell yourself you don't. This debt will eventually come due.

Do not accept special gifts and favors that revolve around a relationship between your child and an adult. In balancing your family's needs—such as for transportation, childcare, or financial relief—weigh heavily the risk that a potential predator can leverage your indebtedness and dependence to gain more access to your child.

YOU, THE ADULT, RETURN AND REFUSE THE GIFTS

Be conscious of any prizes, gifts, or promotions from adults or peers who interact with your child. A parent or other caring adult must return all out-of-the-norm gifts and money to the gift giver. As the adult, you are responsible for noticing when there's an inappropriate present or a problematic pattern of gift-giving and favors. And it is up to you to return the gifts, in person, the very first chance you get—addressing the adult directly, preferably in front of other parents.

Children should not be punished for taking gifts. Do not ask your child to return presents or manage the refusing of favors. And don't be talked out of returning a gift by your disappointed or embarrassed child.

Be steadfast in refusing. Predators believe you and your child can be bought with presents and favors. If they think you will accept, they may even want to pay your bills, your mortgage, or your car note. Your skeptical eyes should fly wide open at such offers. Money ends up perpetuating a family's silence, fear, and paralysis. Never allow a predator to hold your family hostage through their generosity. While teaching your child to be kind and respect others, you are also teaching them that they do not owe their attention and their hearts—much less their bodies—to some person who may try to demand them. Children are not commodities to be bought by an aggressive predator's fake generosity.

SPEAK LOUDLY, BOLDLY, AND IN PUBLIC

Parents assist other parents when they address a potential predator in open and public settings, not in a private email or closed-door meeting. Don't be afraid to communicate strongly and directly about inappropriate behavior such as a special gift. Let your determination to be an effective, protective parent outweigh any fear or worry over other consequences, such as an awkward, brief conversation. Find your bravery and bring up any concerns up in front of several parents when possible.

For example, you bring the new bat the coach purchased for your child to the very next practice. In front of the bleachers filled with parents, nannies, and other families, say: "Coach, I must return this bat to you. My daughter says you bought it for her. I appreciate your gesture, but a gift like this is not acceptable. We are open to your suggestions of equipment she may need us to buy her. In the future, please email or call me to let me know what to buy for her. We don't allow anyone to give our children expensive gifts without our permission. Thanks!"

A predator will tell you the gesture was misunderstood: "I meant nothing by it. She has been working so hard on this one play, and I just wanted to reward her effort." Don't go along with this "misinterpretation" explanation. Just stick to your decision.

If your intervention succeeds, you will never have to find out whether the gift was part of a grooming scheme or actual cluelessness on the adult's part. Even if you believe the gift was grooming and even if you are right, your approach to these conversations can be the same. Speak to the potential predator as if they are, of course, willing and eager to help you keep your child and all the children in your community safe, by modeling and teaching acceptable adult-child behavior. And that you are explaining, right now, what expected behavior looks like and firmly enforcing it, enlisting their help in enforcing it too (a good test of whether they will accept and respect your parental expectations).

You can respond by saying something like: "I understand your intent was harmless. But it's our job to set clear and visible expectations for ourselves and our children and follow through. I'm sure you can respect that we wouldn't want our children to be indebted to anyone for any reason. I greatly appreciate your coaching. Just no gifts, going forward!"

GET TO KNOW THIS PERSON BETTER

If you think that someone might be a potential predator, your instinct may be to avoid them. But if they are spending time with your child, you must move in the opposite direction: toward them. Not by depending on them or sharing more about yourself and your family, but by getting to know them better in connection with the activities that bring them into your child's life. Make it your objective to get closer to any adult who is building a personal relationship with your child. Openly communicate with them. Randomly phone them and ask them how things are going. Chat about their job, volunteer activity, or coaching. Meet them at school—at a planned encounter or just stopping by, unplanned. Ask directly about the time they are spending with your child.

You may inquire: "My son tells me you two are having lunch together every day at school. I am surprised you have that kind of time, being one-on-one with him every day, given all your roles at school. Where do you typically meet him?" This line of discussion should be held in a public setting in range of others. Your tone is friendly and, simultaneously, curious. Why does this teacher or coach make the time commitment to only my child throughout the week? Are there other children present?

You are not accusing them of anything—just making conversation and expressing your real surprise and curiosity. But you also draw attention to a potential predator's behavior as an outlier from other adults on the staff and demonstrating that you're aware of their actions. Remember, most adults who work with children don't want to abuse them, and many of them genuinely enjoy being with children. But even adults who love working with children usually want their private lunch break. You should be skeptical of any adult consistently making time for one-on-one time with minors, especially if those are private meetings.

REMARK ON ANY PATTERN TYPE TO OTHERS

When you recognize that all the students invited to stay for individual lunch breaks with a teacher are boys 11 to 13 years old with athletic builds, you've possibly discovered a pattern. Similarly, if you notice a ritual with one specific child or small group in an organization, mention this trend to a supervisor, employer, or principal. You don't need to report with suspicion; rather, communicate the pattern as a noteworthy outlier, focusing on your curiosity: Why would that be?

STOP COURTSHIP DYNAMICS

Remember that the predator's approach to families and children is structured like a courtship. If you find yourself thinking that the relationship between your child and an older, more powerful person is like a crush, in either direction or both, that dynamic is of real concern. Become extra vigilant in stopping opportunities for grooming moves. And don't use the language of "boyfriends" and "girlfriends" to tease or joke about relationships between adults and children, ever. Keep the line bright so that no one, especially a child, is confused about the adult's responsibility and the child's vulnerability.

The person whose behavior you're watching may be in an actual courtship with someone else in the child's life—perhaps dating a parent, most likely the mother of a minor child. If so, take notice if this romantic partner shows particular interest in any or all of the children—pressing to meet them, spending time with them, offering to babysit, or bringing them presents without permission from the parent. Does he seem to be courting the children as much as or more than the parent? Put a stop to such interactions. The grown-ups should get to know each other well before the children become involved. If the adult relationship is genuine, there will be time later for the new partner to get to know the kids. And if the romance was a surreptitious strategy to gain access to children to abuse, the predator will recognize the wall of protection, decide this family is not easy enough prey, and move on.

CASUALLY QUESTION YOUR CHILD, OPENLY AND FREQUENTLY

At this "baiting" stage of grooming, directly ask your child about their interactions with this adult or influential peer. If they spend time together, even with others around, what do they do? "What movie did you watch?" "What's it like when you two are together?" "What games did you play when you were in his office?" Allow your child time to respond to your questions. If you hear something strange, keep a calm face and body. Continue to discuss the details your child is willing to share. Overreaction is not constructive. Remain calm, ask open-ended questions to gain understanding, and listen patiently. If your child is silent, offer them the chance to respond with hand gestures: "If something I say is correct, raise your hand." This takes some of the pressure off. If something you hear needs a follow-up conversation with your child, you can take time afterward to process what they've told you and how best to respond. Replying with "How so?" and "In what way?" and "What was that like?" offers you the adult time to gather more information and keep the dialogue going. If something is obviously problematic and your child understandably watches closely for your reaction, maybe dreading it, you may want to express your concern, but with only a brief comment. Your main mode in these conversations with your child is hearing what they have to say, not telling them what you think.

The Takeaway

This second stage of grooming, Baiting the Trap, is a predator's way of earning deeper trust and reliance from your family, your child, and your community. If you rely on this adult, they have a special role to play in your life. Save your needs for trusted adults and reliable sources who are open to your oversight. Anyone volunteering to be alone with your child, such as through free babysitting, is suspicious. Adults going out of their way to be with children, especially without pay, have an agenda. If at all possible, pay for the help you need. Otherwise, even if it's difficult, develop an exchange of services with another local family. The difficulty is worth it to avoid being indebted to a potential predator and to protect your daughter or son.

CHAPTER 5

THIRD STAGE : RIGGING THE TRAP WITH GUILT

Predators often clear the low hurdles of the early stages, Setting the Trap and Baiting the Trap, without much trouble. They have met you and your child, found a reason to be near your family, and built trust with you. Any concerns you may have had at those stages were limited and easily managed by the predator. If you're like most parents, you generally encourage adult mentorship, so you appreciate added attention in your child's life from someone who is generous with their time. Your child now enjoys spending time with this person who you don't realize is a predator, and you've become comfortable with the relationship. Now this would-be sex abuser can examine you and your child up close and assess what you will tout, tolerate, or terminate.

If you didn't know much about grooming, you may have missed the subtler clues in the earlier stages. And in trying not to be paranoid, you and your community may not have sturdy, standard protocols governing adult-child interactions. While some of what happens in this stage is distressing and involves real mistreatment of a child, including emotional exploitation, you still have time to prevent assault and abuse if you absorb the knowledge here and act on it.

You must intervene if you see the behaviors in this chapter. If a predator is attempting to Rig the Trap by playing head games with your child and with

you, this stage is your final opportunity to prevent abuse and keep your son, daughter, or any other preyed-upon child safe.
PREDICTABLE GROOMING MOVES—SOME OBSERVABLE, SOME HIDDEN

If a would-be sex abuser has made it to this stage, you are now facing a series of tests, like a gauntlet of high-stakes pop quizzes that you don't know you're taking. Most of your visible tests were in the previous stage, Baiting the Trap. There are a few left for you, though, so the predator can discern what you are willing to comment on, put a stop to, or tell others about.

But in this third stage, the predator's main focus is now directly on the child, to see what this targeted prey will ignore or cooperate with and what will go unnoticed. The trap is set and baited with favors, and now the predator needs to lure the child into the trap—this fake relationship—far enough that the child cannot escape to the safety of protectors. Favors were the bait to get the child and family near the trap, and guilt is what will keep the child stuck inside. This stage is all about luring a child into behaviors that a child will feel guilty about and making the child believe they misbehaved all on their own. This feeling of guilt makes a child afraid to reach out to the safe adults in their lives for fear of punishment and shame.

At this stage of grooming, little or no touching may occur. And most of these grooming maneuvers do not break the law, so there may be no legally punishable offense to address. But the predator's grooming now turns transgressive.

This stage is more challenging than the previous ones, because the would-be abuser is now actively trying to hide what is happening. This testing of a child will mostly be conducted out of sight and away from parents and other safe adults. It is vitally important that you be ready to act on anything concerning that you do observe. Fortunately, the deviations from safe and normal behavior are often glaringly evident, so be ready to respond quickly and firmly. And the tests of your parenting limitations, which the predator determined in the earlier stages, will be obvious. Don't ignore them. If you are paying attention, it will become clear that something is off in this relationship.

COOKS UP OPPORTUNITIES FOR ALONE TIME WITH THE CHILD

The easily observable behavior in stage three, Rigging the Trap with Guilt, is that a predator repeatedly creates opportunities to be alone with your child—literally separating your son or daughter from you and other safe adults who could observe their interactions. The more frequently your child spends time alone with this person, the more unremarkable it will seem. Eventually they may even arrange a schedule where no request is needed so this private time is built into everyone's usual routine. Most parents assume that this is a healthy and beneficial mentor relationship.

SETS UP SPACES AND SUPPLIES

Predators create multiple reasons to be with the children they abuse. For example, predators equip their homes with toys, games, and even home offices for private meetings with minors—meetings that would be better conducted in more public settings, such as on a field where other people are milling around. Not only do these child-friendly habitats lure children to spaces that the predator controls, but later, if abuse begins, the related activities create alibis for why the child was with them and what they were doing together.

Your child should not be entering physical spaces that are closed or inaccessible to you. You should be able to see any child-tempting supplies and environments a predator has set up. Talk to your child about the places they go—they may describe hidden areas or toys you didn't see. If you discover that an adult has an abundance of entertainment for children that is set up outside a child's room, or if they have no children of their own, your thoughts should not be "how charming and fun and generous!" You should think, "This is not normal adult behavior."

Not every adult with the latest version of a video game popular with 11-year-olds is a predator, but ask yourself, why would this grown man have that game at the ready, in his office, and always be inviting middle schoolers—your middle schooler—to play?

TREATS THE CHILD AS A PEER

Another tactic you may observe is a new dynamic between the child and the adult, where the child starts to feel like a peer to the adult. Some of this shift may happen in view of others, where you can see and hear the adult playing at being dependent on the child or actually asking your child to take on adult-level responsibilities. You may also hear this shift in comments from the child, indicating that the child feels sorry for this adult or responsible for their feelings.

The more insidious dimension of this new level of grooming occurs when the two are alone. Preying on a child's desire to be special, important, and useful—as well as on their innocent sympathy—predators add a new dimension to their performance: they act emotionally distraught. The predator has been acting harmless all along, and now they pretend to be wounded—harmed and in need of help—to try to bring their prey closer. They may employ stories of any run of the mill life stress to garner sympathy: a divorce, difficulty at work or home, family concerns, or financial stress. A child who has been elevated to peer status by the predator then becomes a confidant, further cementing their bond. While predators in the rigging stage continue to foster your dependence on their favors and entice the child with favoritism, they also are playing weak, confused, or vulnerable with their prey. If they see the child wants to feel important, predators will say things like "I am going through a really hard time right now and I need you," or "I thought I could trust you to help me."

Treating a child as an adult peer is a common tactic of predators because it works. The child, enthusiastic for mature privileges like being an adult's confidant, feels special. They get a sense of responsibility and pride from believing they are helping an adult through a personal hardship. Conversations about private, personal matters link the child to the predator, affirming the child and convincing them to feel like the one person who can make all the difference. All these factors together lead a child to feel obligated to help, and, worse, to believe that they are the only one who can.

TESTS THE CHILD WITH FORBIDDEN FRUIT

A predator evaluates the child they've selected by introducing prohibited activities—typically while out of sight or hearing of caring adults (which is why your safety protocols are so important). Predators test children's vulnerability for abuse by purposefully offering opportunities to engage in risky behaviors. The activities range in severity from mild to serious: from using foul language to playing movies or games rated "mature" or "adults only," to using or sharing substances with the child such as cigarettes or alcohol. This creates opportunities for the child to experiment and provides the materials to break existing rules. The predator's efforts to distance the child from protection will work if the prey takes the bait, so this would-be child sex abuser makes the lures as interesting and accessible as possible.

To encourage participation by their primary target, predators often gather small groups of children to be part of these tests—to increase peer pressure on the selected child. These peer groups create an incentive to join. When innocent children participate in prohibited activities with a condoning adult or older peer, they are blindly walking into a trap baited with forbidden fruit.

If the predator is audacious enough to conduct these tests within sight or hearing of a responsible adult, the caregiver is also being tested: What transgressions will they notice? What will they let slide? What can the predator get away with?

FEIGNS INNOCENCE

If you discover that someone is facilitating these risky pursuits with minors, you have come upon an obvious, standard sign of grooming. Despite having set the conditions for entrapment, a predator often acts as if they are free from responsibility by saying that the children chose to participate. They may later pretend to have been a passive observer while the child wandered nearer the trap and made the decision to engage in the forbidden venture. Never mind that this poacher rigged the trap with highly tempting bait, ignored their adult responsibility to protect minors, and sat watching as the young prey walked toward the trap.

For example, a predator might leave sexual material in the common-area bathroom of his home before hosting a youth team sleepover. Then he'll instruct the boys sleeping to use only that bathroom in the house. A skilled predator uses a child's natural curiosity and developmental stage against them, systematically creating conditions for capture—an opportunity to pin the child.

CREATES GUILT LEADING TO SILENCE

Guilt is central to this last pre-abuse stage of grooming. When a sex abuser uses adult activities to test and entice a minor, the child may be simultaneously confused, pleased, nervous, and excited about trying on maturity. Children feel a closer connection to a predator who allows and encourages banned activities, but they also feel a sense of self-doubt, uncertainty, and fear of punishment. Around sexual topics especially, a child lacks an adult awareness and is apt to feel confusion and shame—even as the predator is telling them that since they are being treated as an adult, they are responsible for these adult behaviors.

Predators leverage all these emotions to further their ultimate goals: continued abuse and secrecy.

A sex abuser needs the child to feel so guilty that they are too afraid to talk to anyone about the abuse, or even to confess that they've broken your rules. This silence closes off the child's only escape routes. If your child does tell you about something that has happened, be prepared to respond calmly and praise your child for the information. Resist any urge to react in a way that would deepen the child's sense of shame or self-doubt.

KEEPS THE CHILD CLOSE WITH SECRETS

A predator elevates the child and the supposedly unique connection between them, defining the relationship as exceptional. He or she might tell the child, "I don't let just anyone on the team watch a movie with me at my house," or, "You are so special to me, I'll let you have a beer with me, but let's keep it between us." Sealing the relationship with your child is the predator's priority, and he uses these secrets to forge intimacy with his victims.

And the trap is closing. Predators use these shared experiences with the groomed child against them, binding them in chains of self-doubt, shame, and guilt: "Do you want to risk telling your mom what you've done?" "If you stay quiet about what you did when we were together, we can keep seeing each other."

The Child's Reactions

Changes within a child at this stage are likely to take place out of sight of safe adults—either alone with the predator or within the child's internal experience, but here is what's happening, so you can be ready to spot it and respond.

GROWING ATTACHMENT TO THE PREDATOR

It can be stunningly easy for a conniving predator to make a child feel special, to draw them closer. Children with open spaces in their lives actively seek adults who can make them feel important, and an impressionable, accommodating, or tenderhearted child takes the bait when a predator fills that emotional need. Feeling responsible for helping this person in distress, a child becomes increasingly attached.

As your son or daughter spends extra time thinking about this person, they may offer to forego activities that take time away from the relationship. A child may even express how much the predator needs them. And each time a child aids a predator and submits to his demands for support, the predator's power strengthens, and the relationship moves closer to abuse.

INFATUATION WITH THE PREDATOR

Another thing to watch for at this stage of grooming is your child's infatuation with the adult. They may say things like "He is so much cooler than you," "I want to spend more time at his place," "He really cares about me, not like you," "I can talk to him about anything," and "He treats me like an adult, while you treat me like a kid." Look out for any adult who encourages these attitudes and ignores or insults your parental decisions. Adults who truly care for children work alongside attentive parents rather than undermining them.

EXPERIMENTATION

The opportunity to experiment with a predator's baits—substances, sexual material, or risky behavior—is exciting for minors. Providing the chance for experimentation with prohibited material and substances allows a predator to seem cool to a child. A child may be unaware of the dangers in participating, especially if the predator has other children involved. Group settings encourage risky behavior in adolescents.[xv]

Watch for signs of substance use: smelling an odor of smoke or alcohol, finding paraphernalia or actual substances in their bags, room, or clothing, or detecting a change in their personality. Look at your child when they return from spending time with the adult or peer in question. Are they avoiding you? Do they try to hide their purse or bookbag? If you notice a change, mention it calmly and clearly. "I notice you head straight to the shower after you get home from his house. Why is that?" Focus on what is visible, and promote calm, open dialogue.

RESISTANCE

When a predator suggests that a child break family rules, the child may express concern or unease: "I don't think my mom would be all right with me watching an NC-17 movie," or "If this is the movie we are watching, I'll just text my mom to pick me up."

If your child resists in this manner, the predator may reconsider his options and pursue one who is easier to groom. Or, the would-be abuser may up the ante, trying more tempting activities to overcome the resistance, wondering "What rule is he willing to break? What if he is interested in drinking or smoking? Maybe if I get him drunk, he'll participate."
You may never hear about risky offers or situations that your child successfully refused. But if you do discover evidence or hints that an adult or potentially predatory peer has attempted to lure your child into such scenarios—whether from your own observations, from the child, or from someone else—don't treat them as isolated incidents that are happily in the past, and don't react by blaming the child. Recognize these transgressions as grooming attempts, and follow up. For example, any adult who offers cigarettes to your child should be reprimanded firmly by you and banned from any further unsupervised contact with your child.

DEEPENING SELF-DOUBT

Once children are caught in this third stage of grooming, which seeks to Rig the Trap with Guilt, all sorts of new emotions arise. When children participate in adult activities with a predator, the intense mix of feelings can leave kids feeling confused. They feel an increasing sense of personal responsibility for what is happening, as well as regret and shame about any wrongdoing they've participated in. They don't understand that they're being entrapped.

Predators rely heavily on a child's internal self-doubt. It's what often makes a child—and frankly every one—stop in their tracks. What if. What if I am wrong? What if I get in trouble? What if my parents make me quit seeing him? What if something bad happens to her if I tell? What if the other kids hate me for snitching? What if I can't play anymore?

Practical Recommendations for a Caring Adult

If a child you know is being groomed, this stage is your last chance to prevent sexual abuse. Here are your best strategies for risk reduction.

COMMUNICATE FREQUENTLY WITH THE CHILD

Listen to your child. Avoid questions that start with "are," "do," and "can." Instead use open-ended beginner words: how, what, what if, why, which, tell me, and where. Ask open-ended questions about their experiences with the adults and peers in their life. One way I like to initiate discussions is to sit shoulder to shoulder with my child, like riding in a car, cooking together, or relaxing before bedtime. They hear what you say, even though they may seem to be ignoring you in the moment. Keep your own ears open and tell them often that you want to hear what's going on in their minds and hearts—no matter who or what it involves. Be present and willing to listen to their truths. If you calmly listen to the small stuff, they'll be more likely to come to you with the big stuff. Your child must know and believe you are on their side.

ASK OTHERS ABOUT THE PREDATORY ADULT

Talk regularly to the adults who work with your child. In this tipping point stage of grooming, I strongly encourage you to speak out loud to other parents or adults working closely with a potential predator about concerning behaviors. For example, "Hey, have you noticed anything strange about the way coach Tim shows favoritism to the boys?" This conversation starter gives the other parent an indication of your concern coupled with an invitation to discuss it. Then listen for any additional information. Remember that a predator is skilled at riding a thin line between standard and disturbing behavior, which some adults don't recognize. Parents must bring up any problematic patterns with other parents and caring adults. Together you can raise awareness of a potential bad actor and perhaps piece together a larger fabric of disturbing behaviors, overcoming a predator's efforts to keep the dots of truth unconnected.

Sometimes the greatest local and communal defense is a loudmouth parental community. Predators who catch wind of questioning parents and coworkers get spooked easily. A predator who finds out the community is suspicious of them may cut and run to protect themselves.

TUNE INTO DEVELOPMENTAL STAGES

While to some parents it might seem easier to pretend that a daughter or son is as clueless and innocent as a small child until they're near adulthood, sticking your head in the sand doesn't serve your children well. People seeking sexual contact with children and youth become highly attuned to children's ages and developmental stages. As parents, we must become more attuned than those who would do them harm. Draw and communicate clear expectations about what behaviors are and are not acceptable in your family, including around media consumption, dating, and substance use.

We cannot forget that a child's age and developmental stage figure strongly into what tempts, tests, or attracts them. Pay attention to what draws your child's attention and what risks they seem eager to take, and help them find ways to channel that eagerness. Educate yourself about developmental milestones from year to year, and notice what is going on in your child's social world. Breaking rules, challenging previously held beliefs, and taking risks are cornerstones of development, especially in adolescence—the same age when their sexual anatomy and sexual curiosity are awakening. Our job, as parents, is to find and fashion spaces and places where children can challenge themselves safely and take reasonable risks.

FREQUENTLY REVIEW FAMILY SAFETY PROTOCOL

Standing protocols for managing adult-child interactions—including your making unannounced drop-in visits—are the best preventions for these scenarios. Share your family's safety expectations with any adults in your child's life, both proactively and, if needed, in response to incidents, just as you learned in the second stage, for responding to favors.

Build on your foundation of prevention (review Chapter 2 on stopping grooming before it starts) by frequently and directly addressing your family safety protocols with your child. These may include tips found in Chapter 13 on Parenting that Prepares, in addition to resources provided by your child's pediatrician, school counselor, or family support agencies. Remind your child that no topic is off limits and no experience can't be shared with you—and back up that assurance by staying calm if one of your children brings up an unexpected and difficult topic.

The part of your family safety plan most relevant to this stage of grooming is about secrets. Since a child's own silence is the door that can seal them in a trap of abuse, be sure they understand that secrets are dangerous — even when they seem fun or harmless. Even if they're about something we wish we hadn't done. Even if we are afraid someone else might get in trouble. Any efforts from an adult or peer to keep activities secret is a sign of danger.

STAY READY TO ACT

Intervene for your child's protection if you see signs that they are being groomed at this advanced stage. A child may object, the predator may play dumb, and other people may treat you as if you are overreacting. Step in anyway and end unsupervised interactions between your child and anyone who shows the behaviors in this chapter.

And now you are ready to recognize what is happening if preventions have failed and you do catch sight or word of someone allowing or leading a child into prohibited activities. Even though that situation is always unwelcomed, be grateful that you have found it out and can work to protect children from a potential predator.

The Takeaway

As a parent, you are the bedrock for your child. Mentors and respected adults have a special place as a support to your family system, but do not ignore when they transgress your safety standards or try to distance your child from the herd of your family, friends, and safe adults. In this third stage, Rigging the Trap, the predator uses guilt to ensure that a child withdraws from any caring adults and to reinforce the bond with the predator. Minors who are being groomed start carrying unearned shame and guilt over their actions, so the role of a safe and caring adult in this stage is to reassure them that they are not alone, and that their actions were a response to a malicious trick. Affirm your love for your child, and don't leave them hanging without your support. Your presence and response are crucial here to prevent abuse.

CHAPTER 6

FOURTH STAGE : KEEPING THE TRAP SHUT WITH THREATS

Predators take advantage of the fact that they are bigger, stronger, and socially more experienced and powerful than the children they target, and their willingness to lie and manipulate is a hidden edge. These adults are adept at selecting prey who lack an attentive network of healthy, compassionate adults, or who have instabilities and difficulties in their lives.

In the wrong circumstances, any child can become the victim of an abuser. Even if a child has loving, caring adults in their life, stresses like financial trouble, divorce, legal issues, or illness may shift parents' focus away from the child. In such situations, simply surviving the day becomes a challenge, and these are the very times a predator is most likely to appear—passing as a well-intentioned adult. A predator's keen awareness of your family's insecurity makes you and your children more vulnerable to exploitation and abuse.

This chapter describes the grooming that occurs once the sexual abuse of a child begins.

Once a predator has trapped their prey, their stakes are infinitely higher. Their freedom is now at risk, so they work to ensure their victim's silence.

This requires further grooming and a more overtly abusive set of tactics designed to keep caregivers from finding out, to keep safe adults from believing the truth if they do find out, and, tragically, to keep the child available for further abuse.

Child sexual abuse typically becomes incrementally more physical, sexual, and intense. Through the earlier stages of grooming—compliments, then favors, then guilt—a predator has set all the needed conditions in place to commit abuse out of sight from safe, caring adults. Grooming now moves to threats.

In this final but unfortunately open-ended stage, the abuse tends to follow a predictable sequence. The predator starts by invading the child's privacy in ostensibly silly or insignificant ways. Next, they expose a child to nudity, through self-exposure or pornography, in an effort to arouse the child. Ultimately, the abuse proceeds to sexual contact with the child, which can sometimes progress beyond rape to include other physical violence, using the child for pornography, or sexual exploitation involving other predators. Each stage includes ongoing grooming.

This chapter will help you understand what a predator's behavior looks like at this stage. They are trying to make sure you don't recognize it, but if you do come across something weird or threatening, I want you to know what you are seeing. There are also indirect signs, in your child and in the abuser—locations and behaviors—and we should all be living ready to spot those too. If you then follow the practical recommendations at the end of this chapter, you increase the likelihood that you can release a victim of child sexual abuse from the horrible trap they are in. Caring adults like you are these children's only chance to escape a sexually abusive predator.

As an engaged parent and protective adult, familiarize yourself with the signs of child sexual abuse in this chapter. Hopefully, this information will never be necessary for your child, but your family will interact with many children in the days and weeks and years ahead. Maybe it's your child's best friend or the kid down the street who will need a caring adult to recognize these indicators of abuse. Even if you have come to this chapter with no concerns about the children in your care, knowing the warning signs will put you in position to act if the need arises.

A Sex Abuser's Hidden and Predictable Actions

In this stage, a sexual predator pursues their new maneuvers—the abuse—behind closed doors. Most of what you might still be able to observe looks like ramped up versions of the second and third stages: favors to the child and family and alone time with the child. Remain alert to those behaviors—practice active vigilance, enforce protocols for contact and activities, refuse lavish gifts, and stay ready to intervene if needed. If you have come straight to this chapter, go back and read about combating the earlier stages of grooming, and implement the guidance in those chapters.

BEGINS ABUSE WITH TINY TOUCHES

There is no way to know the timeline of escalating physical contact by a predator, but their greatest motive is to maximize time alone with a child. Assaults are most likely to occur away from anyone else's view, but you can look for subtle signs of lavish touching. If an adult touches a child frequently—typically using humor, teasing, or comforting as the excuse—speak up immediately: "I notice you tickled my son during carpool time. I think we can agree it is unwise to tickle middle school aged boys, no matter the reason. Please become an example of keeping your hands to yourself for all these boys. If this action continues, I will be forced to remove my child from this troop and inform the leadership."

Such intentional touching on the leg or torso area is common, sometimes pretending to be unintentional. If unthwarted, a predator moves to touch the child again, more assertively and with clear intention—touching the same spot again, higher up the leg or even under the child's clothing. When the predator has time alone with the child, he continues to force hands-on touch—stroking, kissing, and touching.

Once the child is trapped alone and the predator has crossed into physical touching, an abuser commonly escalates to breast fondling, genital touching over the clothes, manual stimulation, or digital penetration. These touches leave little evidence in the event the victim does confide in a safe adult.

AVOIDS A TRAIL OF PROOF

Now that abuse has begun, avoiding detection is paramount for the abuser. A wily predator avoids onlookers during the abuse while also keeping the physical touch gentle enough to avoid marks on the child. If no one is watching, the only person at risk of telling on the predator is the victim. And if the predator was skilled at the third stage of grooming, Rigging the Trap, the child is already afraid and guilt-ridden—increasing the likelihood of their silence. This fourth stage, with the trap snapped shut, allows the predator to freely exploit the child's fear for his cruel enjoyment. Although sexual abuse is a disastrous violation of a child, it is not necessarily violent. Perversely, sexual contact with the victim is the culmination of a relationship established gradually and based on trust falsely earned. Because the emotional games throughout the grooming process are all the chains needed, a predator doesn't need to hold a child down to abuse them. The child has internalized the threats. As the abuse proceeds, the predator's hands-on touch may be untraceable for quite some time. Because proof puts them at higher risk of being caught, predators save aggressive, forceful touches for later, after the child is even more firmly locked into the trap.

TESTS THE CHILD'S REACTION TO ABUSE

As at every stage of grooming, the abuser tests to see how a child reacts to the abuse itself, and that reaction informs the predator's next move. The approach of set, bait, close in, and snap paralyzes a vulnerable child, like a wounded animal. If the child is confused, embarrassed, frightened, or ashamed enough—as successfully groomed victims are—they will not run away or scream out. Unaware that they have been enticed and entrapped, abuse victims routinely assume that what's happening is somehow their own fault, and they don't know how to react or to defend themselves. Remember, children are never at fault in any way for their own abuse, ever. Children lack the power to protect themselves against predators, and they depend on caring, safe adults to pay attention to the possible threats that surround them.

While the predator's testing will almost certainly happen out of sight of protective adults, a child may describe some part of what happened, to you—a safe adult. Be ready to recognize what you are hearing so you are ready to intervene to prevent a next time.

CONFUSES THE CHILD

If the abuse has progressed this far, the predator is a convincing actor. Having persuaded families and children to trust them, they home in more fiercely on exploitable vulnerabilities—using their knowledge of a parental separation, an ill sibling, or a monetary crisis for their personal gain. Predators remind children how much the family benefits from their help. They also tell the child that no one else will listen, that the predator is the only one who really cares about them.

A predator plays on a child's emotional distress, twisting every story to create gray areas, causing a child's worry to grow: Did I do the wrong thing? Have I brought this on myself? What will my family think of me if they find out? Who can I trust to believe me and protect me? The abuser might remind the child of the times when the child broke a parental or community rule.

An abuser manipulates everyone, both to improve the odds of the child's silence and to lessen any resistance to continued abuse.

A Sex Abuser's Observable and Predictable Moves

You can still spot some of an abuser's moves at this stage, because they necessarily cross paths with other people near the secret spaces of abuse.

PAINTS THE PARENT AS FOOLISH

Remember that when they start rigging the trap, predators begin treating children as peers. When a child feels themself to be on the same level as this adult, your role as a parent feels out of place to them. This is often an easy sign to see. Your child, usually cooperative with family policies, becomes stubborn. The child may say, "Coach Tim doesn't treat me like this," "I deserve to be respected. My teacher respects me," or "I wish Pastor Paul was my dad, not you." Your child questions your decision-making and rules. A predatory adult will convince your child you are deficient in some way—too strict, too absent, or too unloving—parlaying some real or imagined imperfection into a fatal parenting flaw.

Creating distrust and disrespect for primary caregivers gives a predator more space in your child's life. A child who has a difficult home life, quarreling or absent parents, or a sense of alienation is vulnerable to the special attention a predator provides. Preferring the abuser, the child begins to prioritize his attention over yours.

FINDS WAYS TO SEE CHILDREN UNDRESSING

Child abusers will violate your child's personal privacy in ways that seem accidental. They enter private spaces such as bedrooms or bathrooms while the child is undressing, toileting, or bathing. Places like locker rooms, pool houses, or any space in a private residence where the child will change clothes are high-risk areas for predation, since they create the opportunity to see a naked child. The predators will laugh it off, blaming their intrusion on supposedly not knowing a child was in the bathroom, or they'll state how insignificant it is to see the team undressing. Do not be dissuaded.

UNDRESSES AROUND CHILDREN

Another way a predator violates a child's privacy is to undress themselves, partially or fully, in the child's presence. In a locker room, on an overnight trip, or in a home with a low likelihood of observers, a predator exposes themselves. To child sex abusers, it is arousing to be nude near their prey, and these incidents allow the predator to evaluate the child's reaction.

HANGS AROUND AT BEDTIME

Most child abuse occurs when children are in bed, unsupervised, and in their own home or the home of their predator. Other adults may know that the predator is with the child—such as the grandparent putting the child to bed—but fail to suspect the abuse. Or the other household members who would protect the child may be out of sight and earshot, busy, or asleep. If someone who is not a child's parent insists on putting the child to bed or heads to the child's room after the child is in bed, that is high-risk behavior for sexual abuse.

A Child's Actions and Reactions

Learn the signs that a child is being abused. Some of the changes occur in the child's inner life and may be hard to spot—which is why it's important to stay attuned to your child's feelings and thoughts. Other signs appear in the child's behavior and health.

SHOWING EMOTIONAL SIGNS OF ABUSE

Children, like adults, show their feelings. Our task as caring parents is to pick up on the signs. When a child is being threatened, coerced, and abused, they may display uncharacteristic emotions and moods. These psychological symptoms can include depression, rage, anxiety, or suicidal thoughts. Warning signs can also include sudden or major changes in behavior, in hygiene and appearance, or in school attendance and performance. They may also initiate sexual play, age-inappropriate sexualized interactions, or risky behaviors. Use your eyes, your ears, and your gut to discern the behaviors that are outside the norm for the child you know. See the Appendix for a full list.

SHOWING PHYSICAL SIGNS OF ABUSE

A sex abuser can damage a child's body, especially if the abuse is repeated, ongoing, and advanced. Parents should be familiar with the visible parts of their child's body and know when unexplained bruises or lacerations appear. A standard part of parenting includes questions like, "Where did you get that scrape on your knee?" If you see injuries with no good explanation, they deserve attention.

Even if the sexual abuse is not violent, children's bodies are not ready for sexual contact and intercourse, so the child is likely to be injured. If the child is past the age of needing help with wiping or bathing, a caregiver is not likely to see the bruises or lacerations to the genital area. But you may see injuries near that area or blood in a child's underpants. Victims also may develop a genital or urinary tract infection—all highly concerning indicators that need to be evaluated by a medical professional.

FEELING CONFUSED

Children who are being abused worry—a lot. They worry about the relationship with the predator, how to protect themselves, and the impact on those they love. The abuser laid the groundwork for threats in the earlier stages, so now the child is fearful. A child in this stage—with the trap snapped shut—feels guilty and filled with shame, mistaking what's happening with the predator as their own choice and not seeing it for what it is: that they've been duped and are being abused.

All this worry may show up in ways you can detect. In addition to seeming worried and unhappy, the child may develop physical illnesses, such as stomach pains and other digestive problems. Children may begin anxious habits like skin picking, nail biting, hair pulling, or face picking.

GIVING MIXED MESSAGES

Groomed minors juggle complex feelings and thoughts about a predatory adult or peer. The child may hold genuine feelings of care and love for the abuser, which makes it extremely difficult to navigate their simultaneous feelings of disgust, pain, and betrayal.

These mixed emotions show up in mixed communication. Listen attentively to your child's comments about the adults and peers in their life. If the trend suddenly changes—to over-attached, negative, or reluctant communication about a significant relationship in a child's life, something is likely amiss.

WITHHOLDING INFORMATION

Children withhold information because a bigger, stronger, powerful person with authority told them that seriously terrible things would happen if they speak out. Predators are professional liars, and they exercise such control over their victims that a child can't see past their own powerlessness to reach for the safety and protective power of a caring adult. So one common change in an abused child's communication patterns is silence: The child simply stops talking about someone altogether. When this happens, notice and be ready to explore why.

MINIMIZING THE ABUSE

Children who are living through abuse may react by trying to ignore it or pretend it's not happening—just like adults who might want to look the other way. A child involved in activities with an abusive predator may want to continue the activity, and a child living with their abuser may wish to keep living at home, which they know may not be possible if the abuse is exposed. The child may want desperately to keep their life the same, except for the abuse. So by staying quiet, a child attempts to control the circumstances by maintaining normalcy. Even if a caring adult discovers the abuse and gives the child an escape route, the victim may underplay what's happening to avoid the difficulties that will ensue when others finally know and deal with the truth.

COLLUDING IN GROUPS

When a predator grooms a group of children, some of them may join forces to normalize his behavior, perhaps even educating other children to expect certain abusive actions from the predator. Those who are experiencing the same abuse encourage group silence. More than one victim knowing about an abuser's actions could reasonably make detection more likely. But if victims and bystanders have been successfully groomed as a group, a distorted comradery emerges among abuse victims that can guarantee a predator extra abuse time. If all the victims determine that speaking up is too dangerous, their silence further emboldens a predator. So if you get a glimmer of knowledge that such a group dynamic exists—a glimpse inside that unsafe circle—understand what you are hearing and be ready to act.

HURTING AND ABUSING THEMSELVES

Sexually abused children may self-harm, essentially taking over the abuse themselves. This may leave marks that are readily visible—such as cuts on the arm, leg, or neck. A more secretive child may cut on hidden parts of their body, such as underarms, between toes, upper thighs, and stomach. A self-harming child squirrels away razors, knives, or other sharp tools. A sex abuse victim may enact other kinds of self-destructive behaviors, such as using substances, skipping school, disregarding schoolwork, overeating, undereating, vomiting on purpose, or engaging in high-risk sexual activity. Be on the lookout for these self-harming actions. See the Appendix for a comprehensive list.

Practical Recommendations for Caring Adults

If you see signs of possible, probable, or definite grooming, be ready to act quickly, calmly, and decisively—even amid your flood of thoughts and feelings. Here are steps to take.

PROTECT THE CHILD FROM UNMONITORED TIME WITH THE PREDATOR

While you collect information to determine whether the child has been abused or otherwise mistreated, implement all the protocols described in earlier chapters to be sure that the potential abuser does not have access that could put the child in danger. Make whatever re-arrangements and excuses are necessary.

SPEAK WITH YOUR CHILD

As every parent or anyone who works with children knows, it takes skill to manage challenging conversations with a child under far less weighty circumstances than these. So if you suspect that your child or another that you know is being sexually abused, finding out what you can from the child will put all your communication skills to the test. Now is when you cash in on whatever groundwork you laid for open, honest, trusting conversations with your child. And if a predator has made it to the point of abuse, he may have found a gap in that trust, which you now have the challenge of working through.

Think what questions to ask before you sit down to have these conversations. Stick to a loving and calm demeanor with your child even if your emotions and fears are in tumult, and focus on gathering information about how your child is feeling and what is happening—especially in the relationship that you suspect or know involves some level of abuse.

If it is certain that someone has abused the child, your first step will be to set up protections from any further abuse. Your conversations with the child will be the start to uncovering and healing from the abuse, but all of you will need personalized, professional support to navigate this journey.

TREAT ANY PHYSICAL INJURIES

Any unexplained marks or injuries on a child should spark a trustworthy adult to find out how the child was injured, seek treatment if needed, and prevent the child from being injured again. Find out what you can from the child and from adults who might know, such as the child's regular caregiver or activity leader. Bring the child to a pediatrician for diagnosis and treatment—to care for the child and to help you understand what has happened.

SEEK MORE INFORMATION FROM NEARBY ADULTS

If you are confused by sudden behavior change from your child, ask adults who know your kid (school staff, other parents, coaches) if anything unusual has occurred or if they, too, have noticed changes. Don't involve your child in any of these fact-gathering meetings, emails, or face-to-face discussions; for these exchanges to be effective, the adults need to be able to speak freely about adult topics.

Predators rely on adults who fear "rocking the boat" to keep quiet about questionable behavior, so by starting these conversations, an inquisitive parent opens a door for adults who previously lacked the strength to come forward. Your asking questions gives them a path out of their silence, and perhaps the courage to protect the children in their care.

RECOGNIZE KID LURES AS WARNING SIGNS

Remember those toys, games, and home offices from Rigging the Trap? Now that you are on the trail of an abuser, you can see them for what they are and call them out in your conversations with other safe adults, if you haven't already.

Be prepared that when a child reports abuse, a predator will try to claim these play activities or private meetings are legitimate reasons for the child having been alone with them. Don't buy it.

SAY YES WHEN A CHILD WANTS TO QUIT AN ACTIVITY

If a child abruptly starts to dislike an activity or wants to stop seeing a certain adult or peer, it is a sign of a problem that requires parental attention. And you can't assume that the solution is repair the relationship or force the activity.

Ask open-ended questions. For example, "What makes you want to stop playing?" "What about your experience on that team makes you want to stop competing?" Quietly listen to the child's answer.

Don't interrupt with your opinion or perspective. Listen to your child's experience, and don't rush to share your adult viewpoint. Stop after two questions to avoid overwhelming the child. If you have open communication in your relationship overall, your child will trust your real interest in their feelings and thoughts and may come back later and tell you more. And there's always tomorrow for asking another two questions.

ACCEPT THE LOSS OF INVESTMENT IN AN ACTIVITY

It is likely that by the time your child has a close enough relationship with an adult that it can be tested, you and your family have contributed considerable resources to the activity that brought them together. You may have paid for private lessons or bought new clothing, equipment, shoes, and other necessary items for your child to take part. The loss of this investment, understandably, can provoke a negative reaction: "Why would you want to stop dance? You've always loved to dance, and your coach says your skills are really blooming. And I just bought you toe shoes!" "Your instructor will be so disappointed that you don't want to continue. He has put a lot of time and energy into helping you this year." "Do you know how much money your father and I have spent on this sport for you? You are not allowed to quit until we tell you." And if the activity is one that the child liked or hoped to pursue further, quitting is a loss of investment for them too—of their time, energy, and maybe positive social relationships. This is all the more reason to take seriously a request to stop and to suss out the reasons. Many children avoid giving up an activity or sport due to their love of the activity and fear of losing standing—even if there's a predator on the scene entrapping them in abuse.

REFUSE THE ABUSER'S EXCUSES THAT FAULT THE CHILD

If caught or reported, the predator is likely to blame the child—as if that absolves a sex abuser of culpability or made it any less severe. Even caring but confused parents may fault their daughter or son for not fighting back or loudly objecting.

Put plainly, that line of thinking is ridiculous. Place the blame for child sex abuse firmly where it belongs—on the abuser—as you step in and take responsibility for the child's safety.

DO NOT MINIMIZE WHAT'S HAPPENING NOR THE IMPACT

If you find out that abuse is happening, don't be misled by anyone who is trying to minimize it, to say that an incident is "no big deal." Not the child, not the abuser, not bystanders, and not yourself, no matter how fervent your wish that this weren't happening. The "no big deal" reaction is typical of someone who's been groomed, and it's part of the abuser's main strategy to keep the child entrapped and the rest of you silent. The impact of child sexual abuse is profound, and dealing with it may uproot people's lives—including your own. But resist any urge to look away from its devastating effects and reality. Children do not choose abuse, and if we sidestep our responsibility to protect them, they are the ones who bear the immeasurable losses that come with being an abuse victim—losses even heavier than those we incur by facing the truth and changing the situation. Losses made much heavier by our abandoning them to their suffering.

FACE YOUR OWN FEARS

A child sex abuser has spent plenty of time implanting doubt and fear, not only in the child but in you, the child's protector. It will take courage to take the next steps: You've seen something, and now you must say something. You risk losing relationships, positions, and material support that you've spent years establishing, securing, and relying upon. But you will gain something much more valuable: the trust of your child, or any other child who has confided in you—one who needs protection that now you have a sacred charge to provide.

You must do it. You must be an outspoken defender of this child, and you must face your fears. When a child is being abused, parents and other safe adults must act, even though it is difficult.

This is the biggest ask of this book. The time you've invested up to this point in learning about grooming and abuse is a complete waste if you keep your mouth shut and look away. Although you may want to talk yourself out of getting involved or rationalize that what's happening really isn't that bad, this final step of reporting the abuse is non-negotiable. You will need to handle whatever negative consequences you might face for embracing your adult responsibility here. Draw on your adult resources and face the logistics and emotions as well as you can.

A child has none of us those adult resources. They have us. They have you. There is no adult responsibility more important, more basic, than restoring the protective shield around this child and your community. Do everything in your power to protect the harmed child and to prevent the predator from having the chance to harm more children. Anything else is cowardice.

PREPARE FOR THE FULL PROCESS OF FOLLOWING UP

If a child braves their way past the predator's threats and grabs the lifeline of telling someone about abuse—or once you find out through your own vigilance—then the game of "he said, she said" begins. A smart predator has left no tangible evidence, so the surrounding parents and caring adults must then decide how to proceed and whom to believe—and the predator has worked to make it as difficult as possible to discover the truth. Gather whatever support systems you can, so that you can proceed as calmly and effectively as possible in this difficult situation.

The next section of this book will offer checklists for what to do if you have discovered abuse—with babysitters, with coaches, with medical professionals, and many other roles. But the headlines are that you must completely remove the child from the abuser's access; provide loving support for the child to begin to heal; and report the abuser to the authorities and to anyone else, such as their employer, who gives them access to children. Support any ensuing investigation and prosecution, so long as the child's well-being is protected.

The Takeaway

This chapter covered a predator's most disturbing behaviors and a child victim's acute distress. Your job, when the trap is snapped shut, is to record and document all the evidence you can spot. Collaborate with any other families or adults who might be able to validate your child's experience. Predators usually have more than one victim, so your actions can protect others, too, and prevent another family from enduring the tragedy of child sexual abuse.

The challenge for most adults in this stage is to do something swift and concrete to protect children from the predator. Just as the child feels the threat of painful consequences from revealing the abuse, adults feel threatened by negative social or political results. These threats can drive them to horrendous cowardice. It is not acceptable to succumb to worries about what people would say about you for speaking out when children are being abused. Summon the strength to intervene. Your image and reputation do not supersede the importance of a child's safety, and this is not the time to be gutless. It's time to protect children and communities. Now that you know what grooming looks like at each stage, let's look at how predation plays out in day-to-day life, across the spectrum of specific, everyday situations we encounter. Two main factors determine the level of risk for a child: access roles and available spaces.

Access roles are positions that people hold that give them authority or privileges that make it easier to groom a child. Some people's positions— such as doctor, coach, priest, or babysitter—command respect and trust, just from the nature of their role supervising and teaching children, even if the individuals filling those roles have not earned that trust.

ACCESS THROUGH ROLES AND SPACE

Almost all adults in children's lives have some level of power over them, simply by virtue of being adults—grown-ups know more about how the world works and have resources a child does not: money, a job, a car, or their own home. But adults in authority positions have additional power, usually including the privilege and responsibility of telling children what to do, instructing their behavior, and meting out approval or rewards. Certain roles give physical alone time with children, with or without adequate protocols set by parents, the community, or organizations to limit that access. And with family members or a family friend, it's the personal relationship that prompts trust from caregivers.

Available spaces are the actual physical spaces where grooming and abuse happen. As you learned in the chapters on grooming, a would-be abuser needs to physically separate a child from protection, out of sight or hearing from parents and other trustworthy adults, to be able to abuse the child. Even for grooming conducted through digital apps, a predator needs the child to have some level of unsupervised physical access to electronics.

Learn to be alert to both access roles and available spaces in your child's life, always. For roles, ask yourself, "Who is this person to the child—what power do they have?" For spaces, ask, "Where are they spending time together—and do I or other safe adults have regular, available view of those spaces?"

These two factors overlap. Family members, for instance, have a role that gives them physical access to more of a child's private spaces. An activity leader's role gives them physical access, such as while travelling with groups of children staying in hotels, cabins, or tents. So, I have structured the next section around these interconnected roles and spaces, with a chapter on the situations commonly used for grooming and abuse:
Chapter 7, Females
Chapter 8, Peers
Chapter 9, Doctors and Religious Staff and Volunteers
Chapter 10, At Home
Chapter 11, Online
Chapter 12, Schools, Activities and Sports

Each chapter outlines the factors that give advantages to a motivated predator, signs that grooming is happening, and specific keys to protecting your family. And each end with a summary of practical suggestions to reduce the possibility of abuse.

But before we dive into these access roles and access spaces, let's look at a demographic of potential predators that cuts across all the roles described in the upcoming chapter, female predators.

CHAPTER 7

FEMALE PREDATORS

A woman providing care to young infants in a home-based day care center eagerly volunteered to facilitate potty training. She spent her time taking child after child into the bathroom to practice for long periods of time alone. One child's mother called the center after her son began acting strangely at toilet time at home, asking her to touch his genitals and use her mouth on his body. No video footage was available at the small center and the day care owner denied any wrongdoing. The family opted to remove their child from the center, reported the bizarre behavior to the authorities, day care licensing board, and protective services. The child was relocated to a day care center with improved surveillance and thorough employee vetting.

The Risk Factors of Females

Most people assume that women almost never abuse children sexually, but an estimated 8 percent of all sexual offenses in the United States are committed by women, according to research by the U.S. Department of Justice.[xvi] Female sex offenders are more likely to be convicted of sexual offenses against young children than against older youth.[xvii]

Parents readily give women and teenage girls access to their children without supervision. Since they comprise most childcare workers, nannies, preschool teachers, and babysitters, females usually are the adult supervision. We want to be able to trust them implicitly. They can also fill any of the roles described in the chapters ahead: coach, activity leader, doctor, minister, neighbor, family member, and family friend. But we don't always think to ask the same questions of a female with regular access to minors that we would ask of a male caretaker—nor do we typically put the same safety protocols in place.

We consider women to be the safer sex around children because, statistically, they are. If you are seeking to reduce a child's risk of being groomed and abused, the odds are significantly lower with a female. Men commit the majority of child sex abuse, almost 95 percent of incarcerated sexual offenders across this country are male.[xviii]

Even though women commit sex abuse less often, any woman may be a sexual predator, and the resulting trauma to a victimized child and family is just as profound. With women's grooming and sexual abuse under-reported, under-prosecuted, and under-convicted same female predators proceed to interact with numerous minors, usually in private settings with little or no supervision. We must learn to apply the same level of vigilance to females who spend time with children as we do to males, and we need to learn how women groom children.

The females who prey on children tend to follow different patterns. These alternative moves are recognizable, though, if you know what to look for. This section illustrates the known risks: how a woman usually approaches the gradual process of grooming and abuse, so you'll be ready to stop it.

RISK 1: ASSUMPTIONS OF SAFETY WITH CHILDREN

The thoughtless ease with which parents leave young children with strangers, trusting unknown caregivers simply because they are female, is alarming.

About half of the human race is "female," which is a demographic category, not a role. But we tend to assign any female the role of "safe, nurturing caregiver" without adequate forethought or vetting. Across cultures and centuries, we have expected women to be nurturing, caretaking, helpful, and protective of children. Women are still usually the adults who fill the roles where childcare is the primary responsibility (or where care is a crucial secondary aspect of a position, such as teaching), especially when the minors are very young.

Unfortunately, the assumption that a woman is safer creates a risk factor for sex abuse. Just as an extra-likeable or admired member of your community is a greater risk precisely because you trust them more, a female predator benefits from the unearned trust afforded her because of her gender. She can infiltrate the lives of families without setting off alarm bells.

The victims of female predators are often young children. Of victims younger than six, 12 percent were abused by female predators, compared with 6 percent of victims age six-12, and 3 percent of victims age 12-17[xix] Women are more often hired to work with young children, thus they gain the access role of babysitter or childcare provider. A female then enters a child's most intimate access spaces. Sadly, sexual crimes against children six years old and younger are the least likely to result in arrest.[xx]

When looking for childcare, parents often must reach well outside their circle of familiar faces. In addition to personal recommendations for neighborhood teenagers and friends of friends they don't really know, there are many websites or listservs to find babysitters—all of whom are complete strangers.

If a female comes across as friendly, innocent, motherly, or even grandmotherly, she seems perfect to fold into our daily family routines. And a meek or older woman who exudes no sex appeal reads as unthreatening and safe. Eager to trust and sometimes desperate to find childcare, we may forgo our typical screening methods, such as background, reference, and sex offender registry checks. We rely on our superficial impressions, which a predator is working hard to manipulate. Our failure at due diligence deepens the risk because she will notice how blindly we trusted her.

And once she has cleared our first hurdles—because we didn't raise many! —such a woman is well-positioned to exploit a trusting child. Her first-stage grooming can begin right away, setting the trap with compliments to both the family and the child.

RISK 2: AMPLE ACCESS TO MINORS

Because we extend an assumption of trustworthiness to women based on their gender, females have a great deal more physical access to minors. Parents freely grant women and older girls access to private spaces and alone time, including in the child's home or the predator's—the two places where abuse is most likely to occur.[xxi] Children require close supervision, and if they are very young or have special needs, they also require help with bathing, dressing, toileting, sleeping, and waking.

Caretaking women are likely to be left alone with children for these very private or naked activities, while men are not. Case in point: A friend who employs a male babysitter says she bathes her young children before he arrives so that he will not have that responsibility—or opportunity. Female babysitters rarely experience such limits on their contact with minors, and too many caring adults don't think twice about giving a woman complete intimate access. Sharing such private spaces without supervision gives a female predator the keys to a child's body and a child's trusting mind.

RISK 3: USING A PARTNER

> *A beloved career nanny selected new families based on her ex-boyfriend's taste in children. Desperate to repair her relationship with him, she let him come over while she babysat in exchange for getting back together. The two were arrested on child molestation charges after one child's father became suspicious and set up hidden cameras inside the young child's bedroom. He reported his findings, along with the video footage, to the authorities, immediately.*

One key difference with female predators is they often have a partner. Female sexual offenders are more likely to work with a co-offender (46 percent of female offenders abused with a co-offender, according to a sample size of 227 female sex offenders. Seventy-one percent of the time, this co-abuser was male).[xxii] Often, the two collaborate to procure a victim. Women related to or in romantic relationships with male predators may harm children to further their own relationship goals or personal interests. And at in-home daycare centers owned by women, older male children can exploit their mother's access to her young charges.

A female predator can leverage her stereotypical female roles—babysitter, teacher, live-in nanny, or daycare worker—to gain physical access to prey through that assumption of trustworthiness and its accompanying access to minors. She then lends her access to a boyfriend, male partner, son, or ex-spouse for him to abuse a child in her care. Having procured the victim, she then takes part in the abuse or observes without intervening—failing in her fundamental duty to protect the child. People who work with and care for children should not have unexpected, unannounced, and unvetted visitors while caring for your children. They are a risk factor for abuse.

RISK 4: CULTURAL DENIAL ABOUT WOMEN ABUSING BOYS

Current estimates of female predators are unreliable and distorted. A meta-analysis shows nearly 2 percent of reported sexual offenses are committed by women. However, victims' self-reporting of female abusers is six times higher, almost 12 percent.[xxiii] When women abuse older children, the victims are more likely to be boys, and in this situation other adults are more likely to deny that the abuse is abuse. Sadly, cultural clichés condone female predators—discounting the reality that males experience rape, unwanted sexual advances, and sexual assaults. Rather than portraying sexual relationships between women and minors as abusive and dangerous, society often depicts them as a variation on adult romances and even a perverse rite of passage filled with seduction, arousal, and passion. In fiction, a woman in these roles may "fall in love" with an underage student, an adolescent neighbor, or a peer of her own child. Or she may be openly predatory, targeting young males for sex. And reality holds both scenarios.

Disturbingly, in neither fiction nor reality do people always acknowledge a predatory woman as what she is: a sex abuser distorting the dynamics of the adult-child power imbalance. Public reaction to her grooming or abuse is often perfectly backwards—treating the behavior as positive and her young male victim as if he were lucky. Others too often treat the abusive relationship as if this grown woman were doing her young male prey a service. Such attitudes treat this predator as if she were preparing him to be knowledgeable and self-possessed in future sexual relationships instead of what she is doing: perpetrating abuse.

Sexual abuse by an adult woman or older female peer is not harmless. Becoming the target of grooming and child sex abuse is the opposite of preparation for healthy sexual relationships in the victim's adulthood. Remember how stages three and four of grooming try to make a child feel responsible for their participation in sexualized activities with the predator? When the victim is male and the perpetrator female, these misplaced cultural assumptions about women and boys make the mental game of grooming even easier for the predator to accomplish. An older female might be labeled a "cougar," a "hot aunt" or a "MILF" ("Mother I'd Like to F%$k")—not as a putdown, but as a compliment. When we apply the terms used in adult relationships to the idea of sexual contact between adult women and minors, we further normalize sexual abuse by reinforcing the notion of female predation as harmless or as a boy's opportunity for sexual advancement.

These assumptions that women are nonthreatening and that their sexual targeting of boys is not abuse extend the misplaced wall of protection for female predators. They also muzzle the young males that females have targeted, leaving them even more unprotected and less likely than ever to come forward to safe adults.

RISK 5: THE GUISE OF AFFECTION

Too often, a female who abuses a child creates a narrative for herself and others that she is "in love" with her victim. While male sex abusers sometimes use this same story, it is notably more common with female sex offenders, and they get away with it more often. This excuse takes the courtship dynamic that is standard to grooming and presents it as truth.

> *A young unassuming teacher was caught having a sexual relationship with her 13-year-old male student after she texted him nude pictures of herself. Within three days of the illicit texts—during school hours while his parents were at work—she went to his house and initiated a sexual encounter. Fortunately, the boy's mother had a protocol of weekly digital check-ins, where she discovered the personal texts from the teacher and the nude photos on the boy's phone. The mother gathered the information from the phone, contacted the police, and reported the abuse to the middle school. Even in this blatant instance of child sex abuse, the predator insisted that she was "in love" with her victim. The teacher was placed on leave from the school, arrested, and released on bond. She has a no contact order with her victim.*

Get clear in your own mind that a sex offender may label their interest and grooming as "love" and try to use those feelings to justify their abuse.

Their declaration of feelings may seem earnest, and they may or may not believe the story themselves. But don't be persuaded by this claim to ignore her crimes. Their actions are still grooming and abuse. And don't fall for this line simply because it comes from a woman. As individuals, as communities, and as judicial systems, we tend to let women off the hook for sex abuse when they try to defend their indefensible behavior with the "strong feelings" excuse. Protecting our children from all sexual predators, male or female, necessarily requires a cultural shift refusing to pass off predation as a romantic relationship.

If we allow ourselves to believe that women are less dangerous when they fabricate a love story with a child victim, we're doomed. So, then, are our children, setting them up for confusion about what love is.

Signs of a Problem

Just as female predators bring distinct underlying risk factors that may differ from those with males, they also present a different array of signals for grooming or abuse. Women and men may perform any of the grooming moves listed here or in the earlier chapters, and there is some overlap. But this list details behaviors either more likely to occur with female predators or more likely to go unnoticed in women.

OFFERING FREE CARE

Be suspicious of anyone offering to watch your children without payment or reciprocity. Remember that the Baiting the Trap stage often includes offers of help when you need it most. Skilled predators understand that free babysitting is alluring to most families and that we are more likely to accept such an offer from a woman.

Don't allow free babysitting to blind you to a possible predator's agenda. Reject the bait, tempting as it is, and find an alternative. Remember, abuse is unlikely to begin right away, so if you recognize the pattern of free childcare offers early on, you have time to stop possible grooming long before a predator has the chance to make you comfortable leaving her alone with your children.

BATHING A CHILD FREQUENTLY

Any caregiver who finds excuses to bathe your child more than the parent requests is sending up a warning sign. This is an obvious strategy to have the child undressed. If you don't intervene, the predator may interpret that as a green light.

FINDING REASONS TO BRING A MALE

Anyone you entrust with your children as a sole caregiver should work alone.

If a woman who works closely with your child finds frequent excuses to have male visitors present, beware. If she brings them around without asking your permission, this is not the time to assume the best. So if you learn from your child, from the babysitter herself, or from any other source—such as a neighbor or recording devices in your house—that your caregiver has had visitors, especially male visitors, that breach of trust is a red flag for abuse.

PHOTOGRAPHING AND VIDEOING YOUR CHILD

A person who wants to document someone else's child all the time is being strange. If she—or you—are caught up in the culture of taking pictures of everything, all day every day, take a step back and consider the risks to your child. Children do not have the maturity to filter what they can safely and appropriately say, show, and do when a camera is on, and they should not think it's normal to be constantly filmed, streamed, or recorded—especially by someone who is not their parent.

> *A female babysitter earned money from online users paying to watch children live on her phone while she babysat. The onlookers instructed her to touch or move the child in certain ways while they watched. It was stopped after the child's mother accidentally returned home sick one afternoon and witnessed the crime against her own child. She immediately phoned the police and reported the active crime. The woman was fired and charged for child cruelty and online exploitation. The online customers were never found or charged.*

If you are seeing photos you don't want from an adult caring for your child; seeing photos that you would prefer she not take for whatever reason; or realizing she is simply taking too many photos and videos—recognize that as a warning sign. Taking constant pictures and videos can be a prelude to sex abuse. It accustoms the child to a camera always running, and it may even accustom the parent to insisting on lots of pictures and videos from times when they aren't with their child. Cameras are integrally involved in contemporary child sex abuse, especially online. Learn to see excessive picture taking as a potential problem. Similarly, if you learn from your child or others that they are being photographed, livestreamed, or posted about online without your knowledge, you have discovered a real risk factor for abuse.

Ensuring Safety with Females

As a caring parent, you have the job of establishing and enacting a set of standards for all the adults who have contact with your child, including females. That responsibility may include asking your school, community activities director, and religious leaders how teachers and caregivers are screened for their positions, if that information isn't made readily available to all parents, and asking if all steps were taken to assess their fitness before hiring?

Most of your efforts to prevent sexual abuse by females will be the same as in the previous chapters, which outlined the usual grooming rituals. This section, therefore, will concentrate on the role females are much more likely to have than males: providing childcare. (The parent-caregiver relationship I describe here assumes safe, loving, and non-abusive parents. For how to respond if the child's own parent or guardian may be the predator, see the Chapter 10: At Home.)

SEE BEYOND THE GENDER

Currently, the children victimized by women are less likely to report the abuse, and their families are less likely to seek legal recourse[xxiv] To change that, we must become as calmly vigilant with women as we are with men. Females working intimately with children should be held to the same standard of behavior as males. Their performing most of the childcare work should not prompt our unearned trust or exempt their behavior from scrutiny. If parents are going to give females access to children in private spaces, we need to accompany that permission with oversight proportionate to the level of intimate contact they have with our children.

If you suspect a female with a close relationship to a minor is grooming that child, stay steady and follow the guidelines here and throughout this book. Intervene just as you would for a male predator.

PAY FOR CHILDCARE, OR SET UP AN EXCHANGE

If you can afford childcare, the risk that comes with accepting offers to take care of your child free of charge is easy to eliminate. Stop accepting free babysitting, stop leaving your child alone with the person who offered the free care, and pay someone else to look after your child. If you are financially struggling, need childcare, and live in a community without affordable solutions, you are in a tough situation. Predators know it. Tackling the challenge of finding safe care that reduces your child's risk of sex abuse is one of the most important responsibilities you will ever fill as a parent. You may need to get creative to avoid taking a potential predator up on her offers for free care, but the trouble is worth it. Your best solutions will not just solve your childcare challenge but simultaneously strengthen your community's commitment to keeping children safe, by allowing you to talk directly and preventively about safe practices. Look for a local community center that cares for groups of children and that employs good safety protocols. See if you can reduce the cost of a babysitting service by finding one that charges each family based on their income and ability to pay. Try exchanging babysitting time with a trusted neighbor family who could also use your help for childcare, or join or start a co-op with a group of like-minded families. Work together to determine the routine risk-reduction protocols for the group—you can use this book to guide you. The process of setting the safety protocols for such a co-op has the added advantage of enhancing your community's connectedness, as well as explicitly spreading the practice of protecting children from predators.

SCREEN THOROUGHLY

Follow the recommendations below for anyone entrusted to watch your children in your home. Most predators, male or female, elude legal consequences, so a background check for sexual crimes barely scratches the surface of what you need to know. You have to do your own vetting. Start by building a relationship of trust with a caregiver. If you are using a co-op babysitting approach, consider a group interview of any potential candidate. For families sharing babysitting in a community, host meetings to discuss safety protocols and routinely outline expectations of all involved families. (There is a list of interview questions to get you started in the Appendix.)

PUT A STOP TO THE EXTRA BATHING

If your babysitter is giving more baths than needed, wanted, or requested, she needs to stop. Initiate a discussion about the increased washing and make it clear that she should not be bathing the child that much, or perhaps at all. In this scenario, a direct conversation with her is a must. Notice if you get any resistance, compliance, or excuses.

SAY NO TO A COMPANION

If a babysitter asks permission to bring her boyfriend, uncle, adolescent son, brother, or spouse with her when she is sitting for your kids, say no and stay vigilant to be sure she hasn't ignored your response. If an unavoidable, one-time situation comes up, consider collecting your child early or changing your plans to prevent an unvetted companion having intimate access to your child. When a sitter asks, you can respond with, "I don't allow other people to come to the house while I'm not here." You can offer a cover excuse, such as fear of illness spread, allergies inside the home, liability insurance concerns, pet dander exposure, and distraction from properly supervising your child. But a responsible babysitter or nanny will understand your reasonable resistance. If the caregiver presses you, consider your options and look for someone willing to sit without a companion.

Even more concerning would be her including a male without your knowledge or permission. Remember, a woman's having unsupervised time with a child is a much higher risk if there is a male present. Ideally, you will have made sure every childcare provider understands the prohibition on visitors by laying it out clearly up front, among your other expectations, when you interview her—and perhaps in an information packet you keep ready for sitters. Set a protocol that disallows any guests who don't have your explicit permission for each instance, especially male visitors. And if a sitter ignores this house rule after being informed about it, she is not the right person to be caring for your children. Prepare to end the relationship and find a replacement.

If you are a woman working closely with children, keep males out while you are watching the kids. This standard protects not only the children but also you and the men in your lives by keeping all the adults involved above suspicion.

If you are a parent or guardian selecting a daycare, a program run by a single woman is less risky than one with males present alongside the caregiver or living in the home.

LIMIT PHOTOGRAPHY

When it comes to images of your child, don't be shy about setting clear expectations. We've had smartphone cameras in our pockets for a decade or two, but we still have no generally agreed-upon expectations about their appropriate uses—neither by adults caring for children nor by anyone else. Your sitter may have very different assumptions from yours about what is acceptable, and I urge you to err on the side of less picture taking. Think through the scenarios of other adults with your child, and consider when you might welcome their taking photos or video. For example, if you would like to see pictures of your child's adventures in the park or playground, say so directly. If you want certain moments documented, let your caregiver know. Also discuss the circumstances under which recording can take place: Is she allowed to videotape your child's bath? Is a naked picture ever acceptable? Can she livestream a conversation with her spouse or friend from the bathroom, where your toddler is using the toilet? The answers to these questions, in the vast majority of circumstances, should be no.

If you have someone caring for or working with your child, lay out these expectations for photos, videos, and posting or sharing. Be as crystal clear as possible and map out your family safety policy about caretakers and documentation so you can readily inform anyone working with your child. You may find out what your standards are only after they've been crossed, because you didn't know to set them up front. Ask yourself these questions now, and then talk to the picture-taking adult: "I'm realizing I didn't give you clear directions about our family protocols around photos and videos." Proceed to set the firm expectations needed.

USE TECHNOLOGY TO HELP SUPERVISE

In your home, consider ways to add oversight to intimate-access spaces. Can you film, record, or livestream? You can inform a care provider that there is a recording system in your house for security, putting her on notice that you are paying attention to the inside of the house.

If you are the caregiver working closely with children, ask questions about what technology is being used in the home where you are working.

Technology doesn't just protect kids; the footage also protects you against unfounded claims of wrongdoing.

KEEP RANDOM WATCH

Your goal, as a parent working with a caregiver, is to form and sustain a mutually respectful relationship with her, based on honest accountability, openness, and transparency. Learning how she spends her time with your children should include random check-ins, a routine that will not be surprising to a safe, reliable adult who cares for children. You can drop in at home at unexpected times. You may also find opportunities to observe her interactions with your child from afar, in a public setting. Is she tender and caring? Does she touch or caress the child? Such observation is not likely to reveal abuse, since abuse tends to happen at home, not outside or in public venues. But you may gain a better sense of the adult-child relationship, and, if there is grooming, it may be apparent.

Continue such check-ins throughout the relationship, not just at the beginning. If you are fortunate enough to have a seasoned childcare professional, she will recognize the actions of a responsible and engaged parent. Less experienced babysitters will learn that you are keeping an eye out, as well as see you modeling responsible parental oversight. And every time we practice these prevention protocols, we normalize them for our communities, raising the safety level for all children.

ESTABLISH CLEAR EXPECTATIONS AROUND INTIMACY AND AUTHORITY

If you have a nanny or babysitter who works well with your child, the two will develop a level of attachment. There's an inherent intimacy in caring for small children, and they need to attach to their caregivers as part of healthy growth and development. You can expect closeness to grow between your son or daughter and a woman who spends a lot of time caring for them, which in no way means that the babysitter or nanny is abusing your child.

At the same time, for your child's safety, it's essential that everyone involved in the parent-caregiver-child triad recognize the parents as the child's primary relationship. While this dynamic may be tricky to navigate emotionally, especially if someone else spends more waking hours with your child than you do, it is imperative that you deal with this balance at a logistical and practical level. Remember in stages two and three of grooming, how predators draw a child away from their connection to parents and other safe adults? That is the dynamic you are seeking to avoid.

It's imperative that a female employee working in your home with your children recognize that parents have the primary relationship and decision-making authority for the child. Part of a professional caregiver's role is to support the best possible relationship between children and their safe and loving parents. One way to establish and reinforce that dynamic is to clearly state what is a mom- or dad-only behavior. Consider your family safety protocols and provide real-world examples. For example, a babysitter who hugs and cuddles your child is normal. Your child might kiss the sitter on the cheek. Can your babysitter kiss the child on the lips? Is cuddling up for bedtime reading reserved for parents or still fine for sitters? Under the covers? Lay down the expectations, insist on adherence, and check in periodically to update them with a long-term sitter, as what was appropriate with a 3-year-old has changed when the child is in elementary school.

Your children may grow extremely close to their female babysitters, and you can be glad for that affection—just be prepared to set some distinctions about what is just for mom or dad and what is fine for the childcare provider.

If you are a woman who works with children one-on-one, ask questions of the child's guardian about safety policies and behavior standards. It may prompt them to think through scenarios they may not yet have considered. This is a wonderful way to demonstrate your respect for the family and child. And if you are a childcare professional, it is a gift of your expertise to support the parent-child relationship. The parent-babysitter relationship I describe here assumes safe, loving, and non-abusive parents, as most are. For how to respond when the child's own parent or guardian may be grooming or sexually abusing their son or daughter, see Chapter 10, At Home.

SET FIRM RULES ABOUT CONTACT WITH OTHERS

Female caregivers may expect to add their young charges into their own family network, inviting your child for special family events or time at their personal home, where they will meet other children or adults. This is not necessarily troubling; however, parents who have female employees working with their children should be alert to any efforts to separate them from their parents or remove them from the home or time with their own family.

As always, keep in mind that a child is vulnerable when their trusted adults bring other adults or peers onto the scene. Be sure to set clear policies with a babysitter about when and where your child can go and who can be present.

> **Help! When you find out about abuse by a female predator**
> - Remove her from any work with your child or inside your home and discontinue all communication
> - Remove your child from any program where the female predator works, unless she is immediately removed
> - Report the abuse to the authorities and any regulatory agency where she holds a license to caretake
> - Report the abuse to her employer or agency

Your Risk Reduction Checklist with Females
- Screen all applicants thoroughly
- Check names against the sex offender registry
- Use available background checks and references
- Call her references to confirm her employment history and work performance, especially child-related work
- Conduct an in-person interview
- Ask questions relating to general and specific safety concerns that could arise while attending to your child
- Ask how she would respond in sample scenarios, including situations with higher risk for grooming or abuse (for example, neighbor invites the children to run through the sprinklers with their swimsuits off; a sibling opens the door on another child using the toilet; her boyfriend got off work early and wants to keep her company at your home with the kids)
- If you hire her, discuss any surveillance technology that you are using for her protection and the child's. An employee with objections to such a system may not be a good fit for your family
- Openly discuss family safety policies, especially concerning visitors and companions, photos, videotaping, and posting images online
- Pay attention to your child's sudden or dramatic behavior changes as the relationship progresses

CHAPTER 8

PEERS

Three sophomore friends attended a sleepover after a school sponsored dance. One boy brought alcohol from his house. After one of the boy's passed out, another undid his pants and fondled him while the remaining boy filmed it on his smartphone. The video was messaged to the unconscious boy's girlfriend. The next day he discovered the messages about the video. Distraught and embarrassed, he took a bottle of pain pills in a suicide attempt. At the hospital, his parents reviewed his phone. After watching the video, they informed the mental health professionals at the hospital, contacted the police, and informed the school.

Children need to be able to grow and mature without fearfulness; this freedom is a linchpin for healthy development. A hallmark of childhood is the ability to interact with similarly aged peers in private spaces—like sleepovers and playdates.

That said, the fastest growing predator group committing child sexual abuse is youth. Forty percent of all alleged child sexual abuse cases are perpetrated by minors.[xxv] If you understand how peers groom peers for abuse, you will be better able to protect your child.

Risk Factors with Peers

Once children are old enough to not need direct adult supervision at every waking moment, they play together alone, with adults just nearby. This alone time creates the access space for abuse, and the presumed intimacy of childhood friendship creates an access role.

If a peer wants to establish dominance, they can use sexuality to target their peer. A child who holds some power—possibly through greater physical size, age, maturity, academic intelligence, or social or financial status—leverages their influence to force another child into a sexual situation, just like adult predators. Sexual abuse between minors is about humiliation, about pushing someone down. With smartphone cameras, internet access, and social media, the capacity for humiliation expands exponentially.

RISK FACTOR 1: SEXUALIZED CONTENT ONLINE

With children spending anywhere from six to nine hours online a day, they see hundreds, if not thousands, of provocative ads and images. Sexualized content has become so common that it is increasingly challenging for caring adults to prevent a child from seeing illicit material. Weak parental monitoring on devices heightens the risk that a child will view shocking and traumatizing images—including pornography.

Pornography is frighteningly prolific, and children see it early, easily, and often. The free website Pornhub, for example, has more monthly visitors than Netflix, Twitter, and Amazon combined.[xxvi] Greedy for an audience to sell to their advertisers, porn sites offer free access without requiring a credit card or other proof of adulthood. And while the sites build in the "protection" of requiring users to click an "I am 18" checkbox, it is a laughably insufficient barrier against children seeing harmful content. A curious minor with open internet access can search, find, and download pornography any hour of any day of the year.

This readily accessible, free sexual content is the backdrop to the growing peer-on-peer sexual abuse scene.

On average, a child's first exposure to online pornography is by 12 years old, and some as early as seven years old.[xxvii] That means by the time the average child gets their first smartphone at age 10, they have already seen pornography.[xxviii] Children access sexually explicit material through handheld devices or even through internet-connected game consoles and school computers with insufficient protections. Even if your child is not online, a peer on the bus or at practice or on the playground can show them harmful content.

Some may think that pornography is harmless. I'm here to tell you otherwise. Overtly sexualized content online has drastically skewed adolescent sexual development, contributed to child mental illness and teen pregnancy, and distorted sexual expectations.[xxix] Pornography routinely depicts violence against women, so sexual abuse—whether in the role of abuser or victim—can be set up as the norm in children's minds for sexual behavior.[xxx] Then young predators imitate the sexualized scenes they have seen.

RISK FACTOR 2: LACK OF VALUE CENTERED SEXUAL EDUCATION

In the absence of adult-guided, comprehensive sexual education, children have few options for finding accurate information about sex. Curious about sex, children would often rather go online than come to you. Without adequate protections, this internet exploration often makes pornography the makeshift educator.

Girls in their preteens now remark how they watch pornography to prepare for what a guy will expect from them during sex. Eighty-eight percent of pornography shows women in violent sexual experiences, setting young girls up to become voluntary abuse victims.[xxxi] For all the talk of female empowerment, a laissez-faire attitude toward youth exposure to explicit content utterly overrides any efforts to educate young girls and boys about healthy sexual relationships.

We should not be surprised that children use videos as their example for how to treat and be treated by one another when it comes to sex. We should instead be vigilant about actively and regularly educating them about healthy, age-appropriate values surrounding sex, intimacy, and consent.

If you start young, with simple talks about the human body, the gradual transition into talking about sexuality with your child eases as they mature. Don't wait for them to bring up sex; keep the topic open for sharing information and questions. And if your child is close to age nine or getting any type of device, start the conversation about sex and sexual content today.

RISK FACTOR 3: PHONES WITH CAMERAS AND CONSTANT PICTURE SHARING

Personal cameras and constant internet access can turn private spaces into center stage for spontaneous performance art—and for sexual abuse. Cameras and video recording devices allow children to photograph their peers and post material that exists forever.

Children get accustomed to posing for photos and sharing personal images from the minute they are born. By the time their child is 13, the average parent has shared over 1,300 pictures and videos of their child online.[xxxii]

And in today's social media environment, that online image is currency. If proud parents have created a child's online presence before their first birthday, that library of posts is already part of the family brand. Before the child can even speak, they are a mini-company of sorts, with an image—literal and figurative, shaped and circulated. They have a brand. When this is taken to the extreme, the child is a commodity.

Amidst all this photo saturation, children are growing up in a sexually saturated world with explicit material readily available online. They then can normalize and rationalize the creation of their own nude, naked, or semi-naked photography and videography. Bedrooms and bathrooms— these private and intimate spaces that your grooming-prevention strategies taught you to protect so carefully from predators—are the main site for kids creating pictures of themselves, whether the images are sexual or not. Girls in the highest-risk demographic for sexual abuse spend hours curating the right backdrop, filter, and makeup for these shoots in their bedrooms. And in some of their videos, taking cues from what they have learned online, they seek to appear older and sexy.

A sexual image or video in the hands of a malicious peer is a tool for domination and humiliation. Images that were made by romantic part- ners during a time of closeness can become weaponized during a fight or argument. Revenge porn—the intentional publishing and distribution of explicit footage of another without permission—flies out over social media accounts, causing maximum harm to the victim. The content gets spread, downloaded, captured in screenshots. Like spilled flour, the spread of internet peer-on-peer abuse is messy and nearly impossible to clean up. Many parents think giving a child a smartphone is a safety move, but do not underestimate the risks involved in having a phone and being with friends who have them. Sending a child away from well-supervised environment with a phone can solve one set of problems, but create another.

RISK FACTOR 4: AGE GAPS

Children are at high risk for abuse from peers due to their lack of awareness of privacy, body knowledge, and sex. An older child—even by one or two years—or one who has had increased exposure to adult material, can trick a younger child. Keep similarly aged children together with adequate supervision. (See Chapter 13 for more instructions on communication basics.)

Since age difference matters much more in children than adults, a year or two difference could be dramatic. Keep in mind, the average age of a juvenile offender is 14 years old.[xxxiii]

RISK FACTOR 5: CONSTANT INTERNET ACCESS

With smart devices, children and teens are constantly connected—not just to you or to safe friends but to countless bad actors through the internet. Even without a data plan, they have free Wi-Fi in schools, restaurants, libraries, and homes. Common Sense Media reports that teens spend nine hours online a day, and eight- to 12-year-olds average six hours. The pandemic has only increased these averages.[xxxiv] During these long spells of connectedness, children view, share, and comment on social platforms with a wide range of privacy settings, some of which are weak by design— because these companies want to profit off our children, not protect them. Parents with a desire to protect their children through active monitoring face not only pushback from their own children but opposition from the iron will and lax policies of the dominant tech companies. For all their empty platitudes vowing otherwise, the executives of these platforms use all available means, legal and financial, to resist oversight of their practices, thus avoiding adequate surveillance of child sex abuse content.

Signs of a Problem

DRAMATIC CHANGE IN PEER GROUP

If your child suddenly cuts off a friend or group, create space to discuss the situation. Gently question why. Do more listening than usual here. The information will come when you make yourself available and quiet.

SIGNS OF SELF HARM

Any indications of self-harm require your immediate attention and action. Pay attention to sudden changes in your child's eating habits, bathing rituals, dressing routine, mood, and appearance for signs of self-harm. Check the Appendix for a list of what to look for in your child.

ISOLATION OR DEPRESSION

Sudden disinterest in sports, activities, school, and hobbies is a sign of a problem. If your child remains locked away from others, including previous friends and peers, you need to question what is happening. You might say, "I've noticed you aren't attending band after school anymore. Why is that?" If necessary, reach out to any activity or sports staff to follow up and gather more information. When you can, bring that information to your child for further discussion. "I spoke to Coach Jane, and she said one of your teammates was bullying you on the court last week. I can see why that would make you want to quit basketball. What can you tell me about your relationship with this teammate?" If your child's disinterest becomes chronic, speak to a professional for an assessment.

Ensuring Safety in Peer Relationships

COMMUNICATE CLEARLY WITH OTHER PARENTS

Prepare your child for peer play by talking about your expectations. Communicate with the peer's parent: A quick email, text, or phone call to discuss logistics of the time the children spend together outlines adult expectations. Inform parents of your family's protocol when their child comes to your home. (For example, any child visiting my home leaves their cell phone in a public container by the door.)

When your child goes to another family's home, initiate conversation with the supervising parent to address the basics. Who will be home when my child is there? Will there be any visitors? How are devices monitored and supervised during tech time?

These conversations set the stage for visits and help parents make informed decisions, and clearly identifying expectations is the best way to avoid misunderstanding.

In the event of a suspicious event between minors, communicate the facts to the child's parent immediately. If the aggressor child is not your own child, anticipate some pushback. All parents struggle to recognize the flaws of their children, so prepare for this mindset as you strategize your approach. Also, take time to recognize the challenge that parent faces in hearing you, responding to the situation, and preventing any further abuse.

LIMIT DEVICES AND SCREENS

When you host a child at your home, have a no-phones/no-tablets policy. Avoid using tech as a connection tool. Instead, send the kids outdoors or have them find an old-school way to stay busy in a common, easily observable space.

If your children are older, keep them in a large space and avoid bedrooms. Organize an event where hands are required, like a water balloon fight or sports game outside, or a television-projected group video game. When your child goes to a friend's house, direct supervision becomes the job of another adult. Ask questions of the parents in that home to assess the fit. If you are uncomfortable asking them about guns, screens, drugs and alcohol, and supervision, you are not ready to let your child go to their home. Practice your questions on close families, and build a collection of like-minded parents who are comfortable insisting on safety for their children.

APPLY PROTECTIONS ON DEVICES AND APPS

We can make the time our children spend online safer by preventing exposure to illicit content. Anything that goes online—game consoles, cell phones, tablets, laptops, and computers—needs protections.
Use the safety settings on your computers and devices to block illicit content. Shift your search engines to "safe search" mode. Routinely check

your child's browser history for sexualized search words or other words, like breastfeeding and walking the dog (slang term for sex), which may be indirect paths to adult content. Make sure all social media accounts for minors are set to private and all contacts are known peers or adults. Look at your child's photos often, including photos they receive. And regularly review all apps on a minor's devices, since several apps are unmonitorable even with robust parental control software. Furthermore, some apps are designed to fool caregivers and provide children a means of evading parental oversights. Sites like Common Sense Media offer a wide range of up-to-date information on technology for parents.

Although the climate seems daunting, caring adults making intentional decisions can help protect young people.

KEEP CHILDREN WHERE YOU CAN SEE THEM

Like an adult predator selecting a child, minor predators pick the low-hanging fruit. Make peer abuse less likely by supervising all children in your home during visits. Don't let them wander off into isolated settings. Randomly bring them food to get close to the conversation. Be visible. Your child and their guests should be aware that you are physically nearby. You're not trying to join the kids; you're using your parental presence to deter abuse.

ENCOURAGE THE OUTDOORS

Abuse is less likely outside, so encourage children to play in a central outdoor space. Between balls, bats, and bases, children of all ages can occupy themselves. Being outside is not a panacea, though. Supervision is still necessary, and when I talk about supervising, I mean have your child in view.

> *A 10-year-old child offered to pay a five-year-old boy five dollars to undress in the woods outside his house. While the supervising parents were outside, the children went out of sight and the five-year-old took his clothes off. The parental intent to supervise was insufficient.*

LISTEN REGULARLY TO EVERYTHING

After grooming or abuse surfaces, victims often say they didn't want to tell because the abuser was loved or respected. Tell your child, "There is nothing you can't ask or tell me about, no matter who is involved." This last part is critical and increases the likelihood that your child will tell you about abuse. Invite them to tell you anything, no matter if the person involved is inside your family, well loved, or adored by your child. The way I say this to my children is that "No topic is off limits."

Be the landing pad for your child. Make sure your child knows you love them. Create quiet times for eye-to-eye communication. See Chapter 13 on Parenting that Prepares, for more information on communication how-tos.

Especially with peer relationships, discuss with your child ways to uphold their individual morals and values in the face of peer pressure. If a child is being bullied or humiliated, get your child out of the situation and notify an adult or authority figure. Sex abuse among peers is a pernicious and perverse form of bullying, and it takes courage to stand up to predators. Help your child come up with several ways to prevent, avoid, or escape a situation where someone could be harmed.

A Note About Abuse at a School or Organization

Children experiencing abuse at school have several supports that may not be available surrounding an incident in someone's home. If the abuse occurs at school, inform the classroom teacher, assistant principal and principal, local law enforcement authorities, and the local child protective services agency, providing the name of the child and all known details of the abuse. Teachers and school staff are mandated reporters and legally required to inform the authorities in short order; the exact time requirement varies from state to state.[xxxv] Each school may have their own standards for handling events of this nature that occur on campus and during school hours.

Private organizations or private schools have been known to present challenges if administrators prefer an internal system for handling incidents of abuse. Reporting abuse in private schools may expose infrastructural inadequacies, thereby jeopardizing public opinion, individual academic futures, and financial support. Sadly, reporting abuse also can alienate families from entire communities, even when it is preventing further sexual abuses. Prepare for the possibility that your child may be better off leaving a school as a result of how it handles this crisis.

Encountering a paralyzed or even obstructionist administration makes it even more important to notify law enforcement and child protective services of the abuse. In some cases, you may even need to consider legal action against the school, the predatory peer, or the guardians of the abusive child.

If you are an administrator within a private school or organization, follow all mandated reporting standards. To do otherwise is against the law and can result in criminal prosecution.

Help! When you find out about abuse by your child's peer
- Listen to your child and get all the facts
- Report the abuse to law enforcement authorities and child protective agency immediately
- Inform any school or organization where the abuser accesses your child
- Unfriend and block the peer online, deterring bullying by the peer and any sympathizers
- Keep watch for signs of self-harm or suicidality in your child (See the Appendix for a list)
- Depending on the action of the family and school or organization, remove your child completely
- Hire an attorney if no action is taken by the school or organization

Your Risk Reduction Checklist with Peers
- Meet guardians and parents of your child's close friends
- Communicate expectations clearly to parents
- Ask parents about the safety protocols in their homes (guns, visitors, screens, drugs and alcohol, unsupervised time) before you let your child visit
- Schedule peer time in outdoor or public venues
- Actively supervise children, keeping them in your line of sight
- Randomly drop in with food or drinks for the children
- Restrict screens and devices when children visit your home, including another child's phone
- Apply restrictions and monitoring software on your home internet and any connected device you own that is used in or out of your home

CHAPTER 9

DOCTORS AND RELIGIOUS STAFF

A twelve-year-old girl refused to go to her physical therapy appointment. Her mother used open communication techniques to explore why the girl didn't want to go. The daughter said she felt sick to her stomach with him and then showed her mother how the therapist touched her during her previous appointment. Her mother contacted the authorities, the employer, and the medical licensing board, but there was insufficient evidence for any legal action.

Risk Factors in Medical Settings

Physicians and their staff have a unique and vital role in preventing child abuse, but medical settings also pose realistic safety concerns. Healthy children regularly visit medical professionals for well checks and assessments. Attuned parents keenly evaluate medical experts, observe their behavior, and communicate clearly.

RISK FACTOR 1: PRIVACY PLEASE

Adults in medical settings are a potential risk to minor and adolescent children because the service is performed in private settings and under the umbrella of health and wellness. Parents defer to medical professionals for the correct guidance and intervention for their child. Pediatricians see and touch naked children. Alert parents attending doctor's visits can reduce the risk of abuse.

Selecting a safe physician is your first step. Do your homework before you decide on a care provider. Statistically, a female physician might pose a lower risk than a male physician. You or your child may have a strong preference about whether to see a male or a female doctor. Sometimes you won't have any options and will have to apply common-sense safety measures. Check the tips below for concrete ways to decrease the risk of abuse during appointments.

RISK FACTOR 2: INDEPENDENT PATIENT

Medical settings presume respect and privacy. Federal law requires children at age 13 and 18 to authorize guardians to participate in their medical care in order to protect their privacy. Doctors encourage autonomy in a maturing child, and this makes sense to parents and caring adults. In certain settings, a child may speak more freely about sensitive topics if a caregiver is out of the room.

How can you be sure a child is ready to experience the appointment without you, and that the doctor isn't exploiting an opportunity? You know your child. Use your best judgment, assess the relationship with the medical provider, and trust your child to help make the decision about solo appointments. If you decide your child should be seen alone, discuss it first with your child. Do they feel confident enough to speak up for themselves alone in the room?

When attending medical appointments with your minor children, position yourself in the room to see the doctor, the staff members, and your child. As a middle ground, part of the medical visit could be alone, or you can request that another staff member stay in the room with your child and the doctor. The medical practice should help you ensure that your child is safe during appointments.

RISK FACTOR 3: MEDICAL MUMBO-JUMBO

Doctors and medical staff may not always adequately explain terms and procedures. Parents and caring adults are vulnerable simply because of their inexperience with medical terms and protocol. If a doctor says a child needs a certain treatment, most parents willingly agree.

Predatory physicians and staff can even abuse a child while a parent is present, asserting that whatever is taking place is medically necessary. Avoid this trap by educating yourself in advance. Ask your medical specialist or seek out reputable websites to learn what to expect. You should know what to expect every time you go to a medical appointment.

RISK FACTOR 4: THE WHITE COAT

If parents feel they are not in a position to critique or reject medical advice from a physician, children are in a vulnerable position. Remember: No medical staff can perform anything on your child without your stated consent. Any service or procedure for your children requires your approval. If you don't understand something, speak up and ask questions. If your medical provider does not explain something effectively, find one who takes the time to make sure you and your child understand their medical care and options.

Signs of a Problem with Medical Experts

ASSUMED CONSENT

Assumed trust in medical experts may hinder parents from using their proper parental authority. Any physician working with your child should ask permission before an exam—especially before taking off a child's undergarments or gown. This quick step displays respect for you and the child, in addition to giving a specific medical reason for undressing. If a doctor takes your child's underpants off without asking permission, it is time to find a different provider.

If you are a parent, research what is expected during checkups. You also can discuss your expectations with your medical provider to help enhance a practice's safety protocol. Use what you're learning in this book to help shape a community focused on respecting children's safety.

Physicians, add this deliberate request for consent to all of your checkups. Medical appointments are opportunities to educate children about sexual abuse prevention. Say aloud that you are being allowed to see the child's genitals because you are a physician and their parent has given permission. Remind any minor you work with that their genitals are private.

SIGNS OF AROUSAL

If a medical provider shows physical signs of arousal during a medical appointment, end the appointment immediately. There should never be sexual arousal in a medical setting—with or without children.

DETERRING PARENTAL PARTICIPATION

A medical expert who pushes to be alone with your child is troubling. Medical decisions are managed by guardians, not minors, so leaving guardians out of medical discussions makes no sense. Encourage your child to think ahead of their appointment about what they want to talk about with the doctor—especially older children who may have at least part of their appointments one-on-one with the provider. If your child's physician discourages your participation, seek a new medical provider immediately.

If you are a physician, welcome parents' attendance and participation. Avoiding parents and guardians in a child's care is a dangerous trend that can put both you and your patients in harm's way.

Ensure Safety in Medical Settings

BE INFORMED

Parents must get familiar with the expected services being performed at a medical visit. In a dentist's office, your child should never be undressed. In a speech therapy office, your child shouldn't experience genital touches. If you are told a pelvic exam is medically necessary for your 8-year-old daughter, ask your physician to explain the medical reasons why. It is a guardian's right to halt a procedure, ask for supporting details or information, and return once they evaluate the physician's request. Educate yourself, broadly, on what is normal for the professional you visit. Do research outside of your specific community, if the standards are skewed by cultural norms instead of best practices.

SHOW UP

Parental attendance reduces the risk of predatory medical professionals. If you are unable to attend, reschedule the visit or find a trusted fill-in who can stay in the room for the entire appointment to advocate for the child and to relay any necessary information—to the doctor and to you. If you see a concerning behavior, speak out immediately. Say clearly, calmly, and with confidence that you have concerns about what is happening. If necessary, leave the appointment.

ENCOURAGE YOUR CHILD TO ASK QUESTIONS

During medical appointments, urge your child to speak. Remember that your role in the room are to be a buffer for your child and to be a role model for asserting yourself with medical professionals. When your child is undressing, remind your child of the purpose of the medical examination. Preteens and teenagers are under your care. You and your child make medical decisions, and appointments are a touchstone for advice and consultation. During medical appointments, model behavior that represents treating people in authority with respect: for example, ask about what will be done at today's appointment and the purpose of those procedures.

If you are a medical professional, listen to your young patients and encourage them to ask questions. Part of your role in a child's life can be to help them learn to practice assertiveness, to communicate clearly, and to advocate for themselves.

WATCH YOUR CHILD'S WHOLE BODY

Observe your child during medical appointments. Are they freely and willingly taking part in the appointment? Are they sweating, shaking, crying? If your child is in distress, request a few minutes of privacy with your child to address any problems.

CLOTHED PRIVATE MEETINGS

Around mid to late adolescence, your child or a medical professional may request time during the appointment to address topics privately. A way to reduce the risk inherent here is to insist that all unsupervised encounters occur with the child dressed. Another way is to request a two-adult policy—ask that a nurse or other medical staff member be in the room with the physician and your child. After the physical exam, however, you and your child and the doctor should have a wrap-up discussion—while the child is dressed—to make sure any instructions or concerns are understood by everyone.

Help! When you find out about abuse by a physician
- Report to the police immediately and Child Protective Services
- Report to the medical center where the physician works or has privileges
- If the physician is the owner of a private practice, report the abuse to any medical business partners or board members of the business
- If necessary, have a formal physical assessment at a hospital to document evidence of the abuse
- Make a formal complaint with the medical board in your state

Clergy and Religious Leaders

A revered part-time pastor regularly counseled troubled children in his office. He invited a newly placed adolescent foster child in for sessions. He met her weekly for three months until she was admitted to the hospital for cutting herself. Her journal revealed that he molested her during their sessions, but threatened her to stay quiet. Her foster parents, longstanding parish members, immediately showed the writings to the authorities, informed the parish leadership, and removed themselves from the church. The pastor is out on bond, awaiting trial set for next year. The parish has placed him on administrative leave.

According to Gallup polls from 2021, three out of four American families identify with a specific religion and are part of a community faith network. Faithful people attend services or programs hosted by religious leaders, and the dynamic role those leaders play in the lives of families and children positions them perfectly to attempt abuse.

This is not an accusation of all religious people or religious leaders. I strongly believe that children can safely engage in religious life. There is, however, incredible privilege in religious work. Attentive adults who are aware that predators select religious communities can be better prepared to respond to questionable conduct. Throughout this section, I will explore the path to proper reporting and confrontation of religious administrators, volunteers, or leaders. I will also review policies that decrease the likelihood of abuse within your religious spaces.

Risks Rooted in Religious Spaces

Religious communities can offer families tremendous fellowship, moral support, and hope in times of despair—when they may be the most vulnerable. Children in these communities and relationships need parental protection, just as they do in any other setting.

RISK FACTOR 1: CALLING FROM A HIGHER POWER

Clergy and religious leaders are called to their profession, usually by a higher power, and the role of that higher power is front and center. Religious leaders are perceived to be the voice of the divine on earth. Imagine that power and influence in the hands of a predator.

RISK FACTOR 2: AWE OF THE GOWN

Families are taught to respect their religious leaders, and this respect may cloud a parent's assessment of potential risks in religious settings. A religious child is taught to believe that religious leaders represent the almighty and deserve deference and obedience. This esteem is unique to religious life. Religious leaders commit their bodies, souls, and futures to their faith, and the success of their faith communities revolves around the premise that they are trustworthy. Religious staff may piggyback on this premise, this connection to a higher power, in their daily work among the faithful.

Remember that a religious label or title doesn't prevent a predator from using your family for their personal desires. All individuals on earth are human, capable of anything. Make sure your children know that their safety strategies apply even in religious settings and with religious volunteers, staff and leaders.

RISK FACTOR 3: CALLING ALL VULNERABLE

Religious communities call followers to be vulnerable, to share their struggles and challenges, and to seek support and comfort among the faithful. Sharing private details about your family is not inherently dangerous, but predators—including religious leaders—exploit that vulnerability to further their crimes.

Share openly as an adult, and encourage your children to speak freely in their own faith groups. But remember to exercise caution if you see signs of grooming in your religious setting. If you detect a religious leader creating special and individual opportunities for your child, be ready to intervene.

RISK FACTOR 4: BLINDLY FORGIVING

In an effort to avoid accountability and legal consequences, members of religious communities where abuse occurs may try to convince victims and their families that forgiveness is righteous. This is hogwash. Child sexual abuse is unforgivable, and anything aside from protecting child welfare is unholy. Don't ever fall for the illusion of a predator's piety or a community's pressure to forgive.

If you are a religious staff member, listen to the chatter around your place of worship. If a predator is discovered, recognize that forgiveness of that predator without taking any action to prevent further abuse is immoral. Being a good person of faith does not mean keeping your mouth shut about abusive religious leaders.

If you are a religious leader, recognize the potential for wrongdoing in all people and acknowledge your ability to catch a potential predator before abuse takes place.

RISK FACTOR 5: SUPPORT STAFF WITH THE AUTHORITY OF HOLINESS

Vibrant religious communities have tiers of staff: groundskeepers, choir directors, activity and youth group leaders, and religious teachers. Adults working within these communities are finely positioned to detect a potential predator, but they also may be predators borrowing the "authority of holiness" from the church to further their abuse. (To learn more about community prevention, see Chapter 14 "Creating Force Field Communities.")

Religious leaders who work with children are usually vibrant and identified as cool within the community. They develop child-centric programs and may establish traditions of off-site activities, such as field trips, campouts, overnight trips, and off-campus games to inspire children to take part and continue attending church.

Signs of a Problem with Religious Figures

SHIELDING THE PREDATOR

Religious spaces are intended to be welcoming, open, and compassionate. Sadly, the communities around charming predators are often full of well-groomed adults who protect the predators and harshly reject whistleblowers.

To avoid jeopardizing the greater faith community, members may discount and exclude the family alleging abuse. Whispers, rumors, and stares alienate the people who are trying to expose abuse within the church, and these families are isolated from their religious community. Religious adults who are employed within a religious community also may resist action, beguiled by the attributes of the predator and/or worried about losing their income.

YOUTH LEADERS TOO COOL FOR RULES

Youth leaders connect easily to minors, and youth directors may form friendships with children, sometimes outside their role as a mentor and faith leader. For example, your child's religious group leader may text your pre-teen directly. Personalized relationships like these are closing in on problematic.

Requests for private meetings alone with your child, texting your child pictures or requests for pictures, invitations for one-on-one overnight experiences, or unique opportunities might be indications of grooming. Predatory behavior goes unseen and unaddressed in settings where adults are fearful of social consequences. In a religious setting, this fearfulness is heightened by religious frameworks that include the message of forgiveness.

Watch religious leaders who work closely with children. Ask questions about planning and supervision of church-sponsored and church-related activities, and review any protocols the church has in place for guarding against child abuse.

Ensure Safety in Religious Settings

Developing and enforcing organizational safety protocols is the best method for preventing sexual abuse in religious settings. These policies establish and raise the expectations of religious communities, but they are useless if not enforced by all staff, clergy, volunteers, and community members.

PUBLIC SESSIONS ONLY

No activity needs to occur in a secluded setting with minors, and two adult staff or volunteers should host all meetings that involve unaccompanied minors—every time. This is nonnegotiable. Enforce a co-taught format for all events with minors, and hold all such events in public spaces.

OPEN COMMUNICATION

Any communication between children and adults within a religious setting should also follow a two-adult model. All interactions on digital devices and platforms should be public and linked to a parent, guardian, and co-leader. Private communication between leaders and minors is neither necessary nor wise—for the leader or the child.

CO-TEACH AND CO-LEAD

Co-teaching is a win-win policy. Adults and children are safer when there is always another adult in the room, because children are rarely sexually abused when a non-predatory adult is also present. If you are working with children, an extra set of adult eyes also increases the effectiveness of surveillance.

LOCK DOORS TO UNUSED SPACES

Follow a "lock it up" policy at your religious setting. In large churches, cathedrals, temples, and religious spaces, unlocked and unused private spaces abound. Locking these spaces prevents improper usage. Keep track of who has keys to the property, and refer to Chapter 14 in Part 3 for more details.

COMMUNITY ENFORCEMENT

The whole community—not just staff—is responsible for enforcement of policies. As you interact with your religious community, discuss ways to implement and enforce relevant policies for adult and child safety alike. Follow-through is critical when preventing abuse.

Help! When you find out about abuse by a religious employee, volunteer, or leader
- Report to the police immediately
- Report to the religious leadership, like a preacher, rabbi, imam, priest
- Report to the greater governing body, such as the archdiocese or denomination headquarters for that institution
- Notify multiple agencies, not simply a local leader of the church
- Remove your child from any activities with this individual
- Contact the local child protective services agency

Your Risk Reduction Checklist for Doctors and Clergy

PARENTS
- Research your doctor and read any reviews
- Call the office ahead of the appointment for an explanation of the services
- Learn what is typical medical care for your child's age
- Discuss with your child in advance what will happen in the appointment
- Attend all medical appointments or reschedule the visit
- Sit in view of your child's entire body, moving if the medical professional is blocking your view
- Watch the medical provider and your child throughout the visit
- Encourage child abuse safety protocols, including asking permission, if your physician doesn't volunteer

MEDICAL PROFESSIONALS
- Encourage parental participation in all wellness visits
- Ask permission before touching the child, including their genital region
- Tell the child aloud to tell their parents or a safe adult if anyone shows them their genitals or photographs or touches the child's genital area
- Have flyers about child abuse prevention available in waiting rooms and bathrooms
- Speak to children alone only when they are dressed
- If a child requests a visit without their parent, have another medical staff or support staff member remain in the room for the duration

CLERGY AND RELIGIOUS STAFF
- Adhere to all policies provided by the religious institution
- Encourage parental and caregiver attendance
- Publicize safety protocols for increased community awareness and education
- Create a reporting system to encourage feedback
- Lock unused rooms
- Include a parent on all communication with a minor
- Implement a two-adult policy
- See minors only in open spaces or in an office with an open door

CHAPTER 10

AT HOME

A thirteen-year-old boy told his mom, who worked night shift, that her live-in boyfriend made him uncomfortable when he scratched his back at night before bed. He told his mother that he asked him to stop, but the man continues. He told his mom he sometimes does more than just touch his back. His mother stopped him instantly, saying he should be grateful they have his help so she can keep her job. The son thought about telling the school staff, but worried how it would impact his mother. He decided instead to move in with his grandmother a few blocks away.

Home is personal. It's our most private place, the one we hold for close contacts—family members, close adult friends, neighbors we know well, and boyfriends or girlfriends. These are our closest access roles, as well, and our default assumption is that the people who fill these roles are trustworthy. We believe that our friends are like us, possess our values, and live according to similar rules. Thus they gain our confidence, and, once inside, our defenses are down. Because of our relationship, we already have a sense of connection and trust with them—the same kind of relationship that predators seek to build when they start from scratch. So they have a big head start.

Risk Factors in Our Personal Spaces

Since statistically over 80 percent of all sexual offenses happen inside either the victim's home or the perpetrator's, it is crucial to assess the adults and minors who enter our home.[xxxvi] It is the number one access space.

Since friendships are intimate and special, it is common to have your friends visit your home and to visit their personal spaces. Neighborhoods also are an obvious place for developing adult relationships, as one of the benefits of living in a community is to develop social ties and be able to rely on your neighbors.

Predators leverage every possible relationship in their quest to abuse children. For them, the advantage of befriending a parent is the built-in access to minors. And because friendships are a give and take, where invitations usually are reciprocated, predators seeking access to prey will commonly host functions and invite entire families. The event can be adult-centric or kid-centric, but the kids will be there. Then the predator will volunteer to check on the kids, or he may join them for the movie-watching in a more secluded space. Many people think of these adults as wonderful parents or fantastic hosts who enjoy spending time with all the kids.

You would not knowingly invite a sexual predator into your home, but would-be abusers do not announce their intentions—so you are left with the task of being chief prevention officer. The prevention strategies in this chapter apply to all relationships that take place in intimate settings. They focus on the opportunities woven into relationships between adults and minors sharing personal spaces, like your home.

RISK FACTOR 1: VERY YOUNG CHILDREN

A child's age matters as you evaluate potential risks. For 30 percent of children who are sexually abused, the perpetrator is a family member. Among children abused between the ages of 12 and 17, relatives account for 23 percent of the abusers. For children under six years old, that number rises sharply to 50 percent.[xxxvii] So, the younger a victim is, the more likely the predator is a family member, because the key to predation is access. Young children require a remarkable amount of care, which is usually divided among adults perceived as trustworthy, including relatives.

Predatory neighbors, friends, and family members are therefore exceptionally well-positioned for unfettered access to young children— they can skip right over stages one and two of grooming.

RISK FACTOR 2: IMPLIED TRUST

A predator within a family has a green light for access, because trust is woven into the fabric of family—absent overt proof of violence or harm. Roles such as uncle, father, aunt, grandpa, or cousin exude confidence, skipping the necessity to prove trustworthiness. Babysitters, romantic partners, and close adult friends can more easily entrap a child for abuse because trusting adults believe the relationship is safe.

Skepticism is useful, especially with those closest to your family. Remember: No role is a protection against sexual predation. That includes dad, uncle, aunt, granddad, cousin, neighbor, or even mom. After all, every sexual predator is someone's family member.

RISK FACTOR 3: ASSUMED SAFETY IN SHARED HISTORY

A predator who is part of a family watches children over the course of a lifetime. As fathers or uncles, family members participate in the mundane and eventful times in a child's life. Children are at ease with familiar faces, and activities among family members at home typically operate by a slightly different set of rules. For example, children may swim naked at a family pool party or run from the bathroom to the bedroom unclothed to get ready for bed. The home environment is intentionally not sexual, exploitive, or threatening, and safety is inferred in healthy family environments.

For a predatory family member, though, that presumption of safety is a critical tool in grooming. For example, a predatory biological relative may enter a private dressing space where several children are changing clothes, saying: "Don't mind me, I've seen this all before. Do you know I used to change your diaper? You aren't showing me anything I haven't already seen." The children know that adults are generally not meant to watch them undress, but the history of harmless intimacy with a biological relative creates confusion.

Predators work diligently to establish and reinforce that second-guessing and confusion in children, and even sensible adults lose track of truth when a skilled predator grooms.

RISK FACTOR 4: PATTERNS OF BEHAVIOR

Abuse within a family, though no one may talk about it, is rarely a true surprise to members of that family. One particular family member may aggressively tickle the children, hug with full body touching, and comment on children's physical development. But family members ignore those questionable behaviors—especially if the person involved has power, financial control, or social influence. You may even be told to lighten up if you express your concerns.

RISK FACTOR 5: OPENED PRIVATE SPACES

The joy of being home is that we do not have to constantly watch our children. At home, we kick off our shoes, let our hair down, and relax, believing our children are safe. But adults who believe children are always supervised and safe during family events or functions are delusional. Influential family members maneuver through relatives' homes, or their own homes when hosting relatives, with ample unobserved time to harm vulnerable children. Bedrooms, bathrooms, basements, and closets that would be off-limits to less-familiar people all provide seclusion for a predatory relative.

RISK FACTOR 6: FREQUENT TOUCHING

Parental jobs like bathing, cuddling, comforting, reassuring, genital wiping, and nighttime rituals are incredibly intimate. Predatory relatives loiter during times of undress or physical closeness; volunteering to stay inside the bathroom or even to bathe a child is a common offer. A predator is always scanning for opportunities of access. Even in familiar home settings with well-known relatives, look out for any purposeful actions by a relative to touch your child or to repeatedly, unnecessarily, or inappropriately attend to the child in intimate spaces.

Children whose predator lives with them—such as an abusive parent—have nowhere to hide. A biological relative who is presumed to be safe can be in continual contact with his victim in private, unseen, and seemingly unremarkable ways. One sex offender kept a written log of when his daughter showered in the family's shared bathroom. Although his daughter didn't need adult help, he found any reason to encounter her as she exited the bathroom door or watch as she walked, wrapped in a towel, to her room.

RISK FACTOR 7: NUMEROUS PREY

Since children attend meals, parties, and holidays, a family network is fertile ground for predation, and 70 percent of abusers have one to nine victims.[xxxviii] Predators within family networks have an array of children to groom, and if one child is not easy to groom and confuse, other children are readily available.

The abusers have access to children in personal spaces full of trusting adults who have let their guard down—because they are at home and with family. Several of my clients groomed numerous children in their home and family networks because of the ease of access. And families, unlike a sport or hobby, are not easily dropped. Family roles permit devious adults to access children, exploit trust, and rewrite histories. Existing, long-term bonds paralyze family members from acting to preserve a child's safety, even after learning that trust has been breached. Parents' desire to maintain the status quo and minimize the abuse to keep from "rocking the boat" only emboldens family predators.

As minors in a household mature, they move out and escape the access space of the home. They also age out of a child sex abuser's target age. But the predator whose behavior is unchallenged remains just as dangerous to anyone left behind, and subsequent generations of children are at risk from this same relative.

Predators do not age out of the desire to sexually abuse children. Do not be fooled into complacency around older family members with a history of abusing.

RISK FACTOR 8: REMIND VICTIMS OF PREDATOR'S INFLUENCE

Predators who are biological relatives of their victims have an added level of guilt and shame to wield in their quest to entrap a child. What child wants to upset the only family they know? Family predators tell children the family will suffer if they tell the truth, and those other adults won't believe them or stand up for them if they speak out.

Other common threats are things like: Siblings will lose a father. Mom will lose her home. Grandma will lose her financial safety net. Abused children believe the predator's threats and discredit themselves. This mental torture from the predator erodes a child's mental health and, research is showing, their physical health as well.[xxxix]

Every family exists in its own vacuum, telling and retelling its own stories, reinforcing its own beliefs about itself and its members. Tight-knit families and friends may avoid reporting abuse, thinking that the avoidance will improve things. But adults who turn a blind eye or defend a predator debilitate child sexual abuse survivors and anyone who actually made attempts to protect the child. Sexual abuse perpetrated by family members impacts every person in a family, whether through holding secrets, trying to keep certain members silent, or rebuilding after abuse is revealed.

Risk Factors from Lovers, Boyfriends, and New Husbands

Stepfamilies and single parenthood are at the highest levels of any time in history.[xl] Statistically, women are more likely to maintain physical custody of children in the event of desertion, separation, or divorce.[xli] According to Census data, 80.4 percent of custodial single parents are women.[xlii] This leads to a significant number of single or divorced women raising children without a biological father living in the home.

Simultaneously, many single mothers understandably want the companionship and connection of romantic relationships. Women with children are a package deal, and potential predators take advantage of this family structure. Due to the statistical preponderance of single mothers, this section will describe predation by a boyfriend or stepfather.

RISK FACTOR 1: SINGLE MOTHERS

Unmarried mothers may perceive a new partner's attention to their children as a wonderful sign that he is ready to be an active part of her life and theirs. Happy to find a father figure for her children, as well as a companion for herself, a woman marries or moves in with this man who took such a shine to her kids. The children, trusting their mother and not wishing to alienate themselves from her, voice few objections.

Predators hunt single women with children. This is not an exaggeration. Single parent households appeal to predators because there often is greater stress and financial insecurity, leading to opportunities to provide support and create a reason for heroism. Extended family or community may fill the spaces outside the home, but a predator can seem like a knight in shining armor to a single mother when his presence improves her home life.

A child is incredibly vulnerable while their mother is dating. If you are a single mother, you are the ultimate gatekeeper. Be cautious, wise, and selective. Gather your senses and critically evaluate any man interested in rushing to meet your children. Err on the side of protection and guard your children—no matter your emotions toward your romantic interest.

RISK FACTOR 2: NEW ROLES

When an adult has no biological connection to a child but moves into the same home, confusion may arise over determining his role in their lives. The mother needs to be involved in all respects, and you'll recognize some of the questions, since they are the same as those you asked about female caregivers: Is he allowed to babysit the children? Can he give your daughter a bath? Is it okay for him to sleep in bed with your young son?

Since the relationship between mother and child is firmly established, a new man may feel a need to assert power to create his own place. He might impose strict rules for the children, create house traditions to suit his preferences, prioritize his own children's needs if they visit, or display aggression when his rules are disobeyed. Sexual abuse is the ultimate power over a child.

RISK FACTOR 3: IGNORING OR EXPLAINING AWAY CHILDREN'S BEHAVIORAL CHANGES

If a new partner performs inappropriate gestures, behaviors, or interactions, many children will stay quiet rather than upset their mom by telling her, especially if they see that she is happy in the new relationship.

And if the victimized child stays quiet, their distress may show up in other ways, such as those you learned about in the chapters on grooming. It may be tempting to write off any changes in a child's behavior as a typical reaction to the new romantic relationship or marriage. A woman might rationalize her child's acting out as rebellion against her newly formed relationship. But if moms ignore these behavioral changes, the children learn to doubt their own gut reaction.

Don't ever ignore sudden changes in your child's behavior. Get feedback from other adults or sitters who spend time with your child about any changes they observe. (See Chapter 13 for suggestions on how to have these difficult conversations.) Spend your time with your children trying to understand them, not simply telling them what you need them to understand. Remember, your child didn't sign up for a new housemate. Your romantic life can't come at the cost of your child's safety or well-being.

Risk Factors from Siblings

Sibling sexual abuse is under-researched, widely misunderstood, and intentionally buried. Sibling abuse is more likely in families with more than two children or families suffering with mental illness, domestic violence, or other forms of abuse. Biological ties between siblings typically serve as a deterrent to abuse. Biological siblings have longstanding relationships and witness each other's annoying developmental stages: "That's my sister. She's gross." Growing up with a sibling from the same parents over many years diminishes the likelihood for sexual domination.

RISK FACTOR 1: GRAY AREA

Not all sibling sexual touching is abuse. Children are naturally curious about their bodies and others'. Sexual experimentation with available, equally curious siblings is a risk for any family lacking adequate supervision and clear expectations. Juvenile sexual curiosity among siblings requires swift parental intervention.

RISK FACTOR 2: ENTIRE FAMILY AFFECTED

One of your children sexually abusing another of your children drastically impacts the entire family. You may struggle to even believe it in the first place. The abused and the abuser are both minors connected to you, emotionally and physically. You must intervene immediately and address both children—showing compassion and priority to the victim. If you have more than one child living in your home, use the tips and checklist below to create safety for every child, no matter their level of power or influence.
- If you suspect or if someone alleges abuse among your children, immediately go to your victimized child for a one-on-one conversation. Pick a calm or relaxing space, avoid a busy location with potential onlookers or random interruptions.
- Tell them why you are there: "I picked you up early from school because the counselor called about what your brother has been doing to you."
- Show your child that honesty is all right, even in the face of horrible abuses: "I came to get you right away because I love you and I want you

to be safe." Show your child you believe them and will bravely protect them in a way you have been unable to before.
- Avoid putting the two children together. Make a housing arrangement change for the offending sibling, not the victim.

RISK FACTOR 3: COMBINING CHILDREN FROM OTHER RELATIONSHIPS

The rising rates of blended families in this country, with or without marriage between the parents, create numerous opportunities for the potential of peer-on-peer sexual abuse.

Stepsiblings bring a considerable risk for predation between minors. Sexual abuse is a way for a child to assert power and control or potentially threaten a weaker new member of the household. Take, for example, a stepfamily arrangement in which two sets of children are suddenly housed as one. Unrelated children are suddenly living together, possibly sharing bedrooms, bathrooms, and intimate spaces with limited supervision. These children are at a higher risk for sexual experimentation due to novelty, biological distance, sudden power imbalance, and available access. The two sets of children may also vie for preferential positions in the new family structure.

Signs of a Problem

SUDDEN CHANGE IN BEHAVIOR, APPEARANCE, OR ATTITUDE

Alienated by the predator's abuse and their threats, or by criticism from other family members for not trying hard enough to get along with the new people in their lives, children may react by harming themselves, using substances, or starving or purging themselves.

Family members, often not even considering the possibility of predator, may write off the victimized child as difficult or unmanageable. But anything other than protecting an abused child and securing the safety of any other children in a family is condoning abusive behavior.

MINIMIZING ABUSE

When a family downplays abuse, they cripple the recovery process.

Parents, spouses, and extended relatives avoid the suffering of breaking the family apart by making the abuse go away, not the predator. Even family members who experienced abuse themselves may opt to keep a predator in the family fold. You might hear statements like, "I'm over that now," "It only happened X number of times," or "It wasn't that big of a deal." These diminishing one-liners only increase children's senses of anguish, abandonment, and confusion—furthering the damage of abuse.

Ensuring Safety in Homes

Children who live with a single parent that has a live-in partner are at the highest risk for sexual abuse: they are 20 times more likely to be victims than children living with both biological parents.[xliii] Therefore, single mothers should consider taking extra steps to reduce the likelihood of abuse.

If you have a male companion living or staying frequently in your home, you should set up rules to protect your children. These are in place to protect him, as well. If your partner mocks or retaliates against these ground rules, it is cause to worry.

MAINTAIN STABLE MARRIAGES

Families stabilized through marriage and legal commitment correlate significantly with child safety: Children living with their married mom and dad have the lowest rates of sexual abuse.[xliv] Whether you enthusiastically support the institution of marriage or you simply believe it is a societal construct, the statistics show clearly that it matters if a child is raised with their original parents in the same home.

To greatly reduce the risk of sexual abuse by a family member, invest effort in your relationship with and your marriage to the child's parent. Before you marry, enroll in premarital counseling services and marriage education programs. Once you've tied the knot, avail yourself of outside resources to strengthen your relationship before ever bringing a child into your family. Although marriage is not a guarantee that abuse will not occur, families without marriage bonds face greater threats from predators. Paradoxically, staying with an abusive spouse is not constructive for you or your children. An abuser is unlikely to change, and your children are at risk. Leave abusive marriages when you and your children are in harm's way.

KEEP YOUR LOVE LIFE SEPARATE

If you are a woman dating for companionship, keep your child or children completely out of it. There is little reward to a child to introduce them to every male who is in your life for several weeks or months at a time. These men are boyfriends to you, not temporary fathers to your child.

Multiple men passing through a child's life can be confusing and distracting to them. Children need stability and security, and the loss they feel if they've become attached to a boyfriend who abruptly disappears is jarring and emotionally damaging. Prevent this drama by keeping children at a distinct distance from your romantic pursuits. Dating without your child also offers you time to be a girlfriend without placing your child on display.

As relationships develop, there is the possibility that a boyfriend may become a permanent part of the family. I still advocate keeping your child out of that relationship equation for the first year. A worthy boyfriend, who is not a predator, will respect your decision and build your trust without demanding access to your child.

LIVE APART UNTIL ALL CHILDREN ARE OF AGE

Minor children are at highest risk for sexual abuse if they live in the same house as a mother's male partner. The safest solution, in terms of a single mother reducing predators' access to her child, is to live apart from her romantic partner until her children are of age.

If you and a romantic partner decide to live together, and when it is feasible, designate spaces in the home that are off-limits for your partner and their children. These might include the child's bedroom, a particular bathroom, or another space in the house that could be used for respite away from shared spaces.

When you move in with a new partner, establish rules of privacy and respect. Bathrooms are off limits if occupied by your child. Bathing spaces should have doors that can be locked, but never used to lock a child and adult in together. Address issues of privacy with simple tactics. For example, if your daughter is used to walking out of the bathroom wrapped in a towel after her shower, give her a bathrobe for increased coverage.

Keep your intimate relationship behind closed and locked doors. Your child does not need to hear about your intimate relationship, ever. Reserve your comments or stories for your social time with other adults.

DON'T USE ALCOHOL OR OTHER DRUGS

Predators are attracted to mothers who use substances or have a casual view of inebriation, because adults under the influence of alcohol or drugs can create unsafe situations for children. To decrease the risk of sexual abuse, avoid intoxicating substances or reduce your consumption when children are home. If alcohol or drug consumption is common practice within your relationship, the risk of child abuse by a male partner or his friends escalates.

OBSERVE CHILDREN CLOSELY!

Sexual abuse by a family member can create an emotionally "orphaned" child within a family if that child is not believed or is punished for telling the truth. Turning the child into the problem, rather than the predator, acts as a cover for family members who want to maintain familial relationships.

Afraid of losing any bonds that might remain, a child adjusts to fit into the family environment while attempting to minimize their own abuse. Abused children might avoid showering at home, stay awake at night, sneak out to avoid a visit from a predator, or become aggressive. A struggling child may isolate themselves if the family humiliates them. If no one believes them or acts to protect them, children may run away from home or move in with friends.

KNOW THE INDIVIDUALS IN YOUR HOME

Pay attention to people's comments and remarks about your close friends and family members, the good and the bad. Predators play the long game, and their behavior recurs—starting and restarting whenever and wherever they believe they will find available prey.

When observant, caring relatives pay attention, it is unlikely a predator can hide within the family. Take time to learn about your family's story: Who is left out of family gatherings and why? Are there any family members who are removed and why? Any apparent explanations in the story? Talking with people may reveal patterns.

GUARD BATHROOMS

Bathrooms are hot zones for abuse, and access to them needs to be monitored. Pay attention to adults who constantly stay near bathrooms during family events and functions. Bathrooms provide predatory relatives easy access to intimate encounters with your child, so remind your child that no adult should be with them in the bathroom or join them in the bath or shower—even relatives.

During potty training years, typically beginning around 2 years old and completing near 5 years of age, genital care and cleanliness should be taught by a caring parent. After 5 or 6 years old, when most children can shower unassisted, an adult should rarely enter a bathroom with a child, and then only for brief moments at the child's request. (Don't, however, leave children unattended in a bath. Two-thirds of child drownings at home occur in the bathtub—sometimes in as little as two inches of water.)[xlv]

Educate your child that a lock on the door protects their private time in the bathroom. Make sure the locks in your home work properly, and teach your children how to use them. If you are visiting somewhere and there is no lock on the bathroom, or the lock is broken, accompany your child to hold the door shut or keep others out. Keep an eye on bathroom entrances and exits at functions and when relatives are over.

PROTECT BEDROOMS

Bedrooms, like bathrooms, are private spaces for children. Predatory relatives or close adult friends frequently volunteer to visit children in their bedrooms. This might be an offer to check on the child, tuck them in, read to them privately, scratch or rub their back, or turn off the lights in the child's room.

Attentive parents foil a predator's plan by declining the offer, accompany-ing the relative to the child's room, or suggesting a more-public alternative. For example, you might say: "If you want to read to Sammy, I'll come with you. He and I would love to share that time with you. Or better yet, let me bring him out to the living room and we can all hear your stories!"

Family visiting from afar may try to guilt you into allowing more access by saying they never get to experience special moments, like tucking the child in. Tell your relatives that you reserve bedrooms as private spaces for the children, and direct their time with your child to waking hours in common areas. Reassure relatives that special moments can happen in open spaces. Encourage reading, cuddling, and conversation to take place in a living room, patio, or kitchen.

Even in these common areas, avoid all opportunities for hiding hands and bodies. If people are cuddled up with the child, there should be no blankets large enough to cover up the adult and child together.

If relatives need to be in a child's room for some agreed-upon reason, the door should always remain open, and the visit should be brief and purposeful. You can accompany them or, after a few minutes, go to the child's room to bring everyone back to the common area. And always avoid allowing adults to visit your child alone when the child is in bed. If a child wishes to show a relative a toy in their room, have the child bring the toy out instead.

DEFEND SLEEPING CHILDREN

Predators use nighttime to abuse children because children are more vulnerable when they are asleep or mentally foggy. A spouse, sibling, or other adult who repeatedly finds reasons to visit a child's room at night is a huge problem.

Predators find the sneakiest way to get what they want. Sometimes this may look like a blessing—and offer to take over a nighttime parenting task when a parent is tired, possibly inebriated, or just fed up. But parents need to protect sleeping children. Keep bedrooms private at night.

AVOID SHARED BEDS

All children need to develop the skill of sleeping alone, although some struggle in the early years. Teach your child that their bed, like the parental bed, is private. Co-sleeping among siblings of different sexes should end before any child turns double digits. Same-sex sibling sleepovers require everyone in their own bed or sleeping space after age 10. Avoid issues by choosing the protective option.

Adult friends and relatives should never sleep with your children. Predators encourage sleeping with children, and it is a huge red flag if a boyfriend or romantic partner wants your child to sleep with the two of you.

Immediately confront a partner who wishes to be with your child while they are sleeping. This warning sign can't be ignored and should spark doubts about whether the relationship should continue.

Help! If Your Child Has Been Abused at Home
- Listen to your child and find out all the facts
- Believe your child and remind them it is not their fault at all
- Report abuse allegations or legitimate suspicions to Child Protective Services and the police
- Prevent all contact with the predator, including removing them from the home or leaving the home with your children

Your Risk Reduction Checklist for Home

FAMILY MEMBERS, CLOSE ADULTS, PEERS
- Encourage children to play outside or at a public venue, instead of a private residence
- Limit play to public spaces, not bedrooms, bathrooms, or remote areas of the home
- Supervise your child with other children at play in your home, or have a trusted adult watch the children at play
- Openly discuss supervision expectations with other parents before visits
- When an adult is in your home, prevent them from being alone with the children
- Limit sleepovers. Establish some rules for your child and review your expectations with the host family
- Enforce your family safety rules and explain that the rules follow your child even when they go to someone else's house

SIBLINGS
- Enforce separate rooms, or at least separate beds, for siblings
- Supervise sibling groups or hire a caring adult to attend to them
- Avoid siblings as babysitters, because that situation gives one child power over another
- Communicate your expectations to your children's peers and their guardians before any visits
- Educate your children about their bodies (using proper terminology) and reinforcing that their body is theirs (See Chapter 13 for more information on communication.)

ROMANTIC INTERESTS
- Don't introduce your children to your romantic interests
- Live apart until your minor child moves out, or designate spaces in your home that are off-limits to your romantic interests
- Spend time as a couple without your children
- Keep your love life separate from your life as a parent
- Establish and uphold scheduled time to be alone with your child
- Keep hygiene, discipline, and physical tenderness as your job, not that of your romantic interest

CHAPTER 11

ONLINE

A 15-year-old boy received a friend request during an online sports game. He ignored it but then found the same name was following his social media account. The next time, he accepted the request. After some small chat about the game, the friend asked the boy for a picture of his face. The boy sent one without thinking anything of it. The next day, the boy received images of his face on someone else's naked body. The friend told him he would send these images out to his contacts through social media if he didn't send him naked images of himself. The boy, embarrassed and nervous, sent the nude image reluctantly. The friend returned asking for more pictures. The boy showed his father the messages. His father was able to contact the police and the department is investigating.

Risk Factors Online

The tech industry is profiting off our children's innocence, and parents are often unknowing pimps supplying the product. Parents unfamiliar with predators' online habits can use this chapter as a guide to recognize grooming online and decrease the risks posed to their children. Online predators thrive in the gap between uninformed parents and tech-savvy youth, and we must get real about the content available to children through personal devices in and out of school.

Most families supply cellphones to their children as a tool to enhance safety and monitoring. This shift towards putting personal and private communication onto digital gadgets dramatically impacts children, parents, families, and communities. As children connect with peers and adults through these devices, the possibility for predation blooms.

When your child is first beginning to use online tools, don't send them into the danger zone unprepared. Start small, and instruct them from day one about safety online, in tandem with their level of use. As children show respect for those safety precautions, give them opportunities to practice using online platforms safely. Technology is here to stay. If our children learn how we protect them and how they need to protect themselves, they will be prepared to handle themselves.

Though the internet is one of the main tools feeding the rising tide of child-on-child sex abuse, this chapter concentrates on adults using the internet to gain access to child victims.

RISK FACTOR 1: SMART KIDS, STUPID ACCESS

Parents must constantly make decisions about what's in their children's best interest, ranging from what to feed them for supper to where to send them to school. Whether and when to give your child a phone with internet access and a camera is one of those decisions. It's a personal choice that also has public impact. The study I mentioned earlier in this book tells us that children receive their first smartphone at 10 years old.[xlvi] Across America, smart phone ownership is on the rise with 41 percent of eight - 12 year olds and 84 percent of 13 – 18 year olds owning a smartphone. [xlvii] With this incredible youthful customer base, homes and schools alike must acknowledge a child's twenty-four-hour online access and prepare themselves by learning about best practices.

Your child may press you for a smartphone because they want the apps and social contact, but you may think of it as primarily a tool to help you as a parent—with safety and with logistics. You like always knowing where your child is and always being able to reach them—in fact, 66 percent of teens report that their parents text them during the school day.[xlviii] Plus, it feels like a safety measure that they can always reach you and keep you up to date about issues in a school day or activities in real time.

While this access is convenient to parents, it also is a gold mine for predators. Under-supervised or unmonitored devices in the hands of minors are a predator's dream. They can make short work of grooming, leaping from compliments to bait to threats, because we have thrown the children into their hunting grounds and walked away.

Think of the online spaces opened up by these devices just like the areas in your home that you know to protect—like bedrooms and bathrooms— where you would never let a stranger waltz in to prey on your child.

Predators monitor multiple channels, and they have ample time to wait for a susceptible child to respond to the contact they initiated—the many traps they set and baited with compliments. A patient hunter, the predator positions himself online to take whatever he can reach.

RISK FACTOR 2: PREDATOR'S CHEAT SHEET

Within app stores, the parent of a minor can peruse apps geared towards their child based on age, gender, and interests. The predator uses that same list as a cheat sheet for where to find his preferred targets. App creators' priority is not your child's safety, it is to create games with high ratings and frequent use rates. And as of this writing, apps targeting children are woefully under-regulated and have meager protections that tech-savvy children can easily circumvent.

Take for example Warplanes, a free vintage aircraft flying game targeted at boys age 12 and up. When a child seeks your permission to download this application, you look up the reviews, watch a short demo, and decide it's harmless. So you download the app and hand over the device.

Somewhere out there in internet land, an adult sex offender who targets young boys is also downloading this application. He creates an online identity and interacts with the other players on this app, and the app assists him in accessing potential victims. Even on the most secure devices, security differs inside apps. Be vigilant about your child's apps and re-read any chats. When possible, deactivate the chat feature or ban chatting with strangers through the app. Or better yet, do not download games that allow interactive play and chat online.

RISK FACTOR 3: PRIVATE CHAT

Chat capabilities for players within games are no big deal if all the players are in similar grades and familiar with each other. But chatting, as part of the game, gives predators a direct path for one-on-one conversation.

Online grooming begins as generic greetings that sound like they're from peers: "Hey," to which a minor child playing an online game simply responds "Hey." Then the online predator asks about a favorite sport, team, or hobby: "Do you watch football?", an innocuous question designed to elicit information. The child, not thinking about who is writing to them or why, responds: "Yes, I love the Patriots." The response opens the door for the predator to walk through. Through just this limited exchange, the offender has learned this child likes to watch football on TV and play a war planes game. He knows how the child spends time and when.

As the conversation progresses, the predator may also get clues about where the child might live: "What's your school mascot? What do you like to do for fun? What are you doing this summer?" Children assume anyone playing the game is also their age, so they think they're talking to another kid. An adult, however, can recognize the age difference when reading over the conversation. (More on this in the Signs of a Problem section of this chapter.)

RISK FACTOR 4: ANONYMITY AND FAKE IDENTITIES

Predators in actual spaces have tangible identities. Online predators' identities are completely fabricated. An online predator is a chameleon, constantly creating and changing names and profiles to blend in with minors, and he can leap across the city, state or country with the click of a mouse. Since there are no geographical boundaries for online child sex abusers, preventing their access in advance is critical.

RISK FACTOR 5: OVERSHARING

Children often share details of their life with predators who are skilled at eliciting information with innocuous-sounding questions. For example, a minor playing online steps away from the game momentarily. The adult predator asks, "Where did you go?" Answer: "My mom just got back from work and I had to say hi." Now the predator knows the child is alone after school. If the relationship progresses, the adult knows he can have unsupervised access to the child.

Predators also use offers of gifts and treats to gain identifying information from children. For example, a sex offender groomed a young boy for a month through an online game chat. When the boy broke his game controller, the online offender offered to send him a new one. The child thought getting a free new controller in the mail from someone online was awesome. And the predator got the child's address. The boy's parent removed him from the game and reported the identity provided inside the game to the authorities. Additionally, the package order and shipment details were handed over to the police for tracking.

Children are largely unaware of how revealing their address or other identifying information can put them at risk, so attentive adults need to monitor kids' interactions online and recognize the grooming that lurks in chat language and gifts.

RISK FACTOR 6: UNSUPERVISED MINORS

Due to the overwhelming number of minors on social media and other websites, predation by peers is extremely common online. From cyber bullying to bribery, perverse activity by peers against peers is rampant.

Teach your children that they are liable for their behavior online, and make sure they know that what they post online lasts forever. Use examples of negative consequences for online behavior to illustrate your point, and give them strategies to avoid the pitfalls: Implement a "stop and think" window—a number of minutes to wait before posting or responding to a social media message. (This could extend to days depending on the emotional weight of the posts involved.) Even more powerful, join the conversation by creating your own profile on the same social media platforms to observe for yourself.

Signs of a Problem

Attentive adults can recognize and shut down predators using apps to access children. If a sex abuser pursues a child online, the evidence is in the game itself—parents just need to learn to recognize it. Predators join multiple games to fish for opportunity, so evaluate each game or app's group messaging and private messaging capabilities.

CHATTING LIKE AN ADULT

Children playing online games are there to play the game, not chat about their day. But predators are there solely to gather information and groom their victims, so they typically will ask more questions than other people in the chat.

CORRECTING GRAMMAR

Predators online show adult traits. Adults use more correct language and type faster than children. They may even correct your child—retyping a word or responding "you spelled that wrong." Few children would ever take the time to correct another child's spelling during an online game, so if a chatter corrects your child's mistyped word, you are probably dealing with an adult.

ARRANGING NEXT CONTACT

Predatory adults, in their efforts to keep contact going, schedule to talk again. "Can we talk again tonight at 10:30?" A minor child responds, "I'm asleep then." A potential offender will then push the child to break rules, like not being online after dark or in bed. Parents can recognize this request to speak late at night as a clue to likely predation.

REQUESTING PICTURES

Adult predators online ask for images. "Send a picture of your muscles." "I want to see what you look like." A naive child with insufficient supervision sees no harm sending a photo. In fact, as we covered in Chapter 8, being photographed is part of children's social DNA. They eagerly share their bulging bicep or their makeup skills through artfully filtered selfies.

Requests for nonsexual photos quickly progress to provocative images. "Show me your underwear." "I wonder what you look like with your swimsuit off." These lines of questioning and requests may seem flattering or make a child feel proud of themselves. And if a child struggles with friendships at school or is feeling unloved at home, the risk that they will comply is even greater; the invitation to be celebrated by a stranger online feels good.

If your minor has sent a nude or suggestive photo, do not overreact with your child. Always contact the police, even if the requests your child responded to were from a stranger that you don't know how to trace.

AVOIDING SOCIAL MEDIA

It is common to see children abandon a social media platform or quit playing a game after experiencing abuse. Ask your child why they disabled an account or deleted a game.

Ensuring Safety in Online Spaces

Society has numerous laws and mechanisms to keep people safe. Cars are dangerous, for instance, so we have all sorts of measures to decrease the dangers. We teach our children to use seatbelts, and we give babies and younger children the extra protection of car seats.

The internet is dangerous, too, so online protections must be in place before a child enters online spaces for the first time. As caregivers and guardians, we hold the responsibility to buckle children in until they can consistently take over the job. We don't give children car keys at age 10, when they can't even see over the dashboard. Likewise, caring adults don't hand fully loaded electronic devices to children without safety limits. So, the following suggestions are your online seatbelts.

GET A DUMB PHONE

Don't fall victim to believing your child needs a phone. But if you must text or call your child throughout the day, buy them a dumb phone. While they are getting harder to find, phones for only calling and texting are still available. They give the security of reaching a child while avoiding the digital quicksand of a smart device. If you want a tracker on your child as they move about the day, buy a dedicated GPS tracker without phone capabilities.

DISABLE CAMERAS

Skilled hackers can access cameras on devices without consent so, if possible, disable the cameras entirely. Any camera is at risk of being activated remotely, so cover the cameras on devices and computers in bedrooms—don't forget the "selfie" side of the phone cameras.

Children are accustomed to having their picture taken and distributed digitally. Homeroom teachers, parents at most events and non-events, and friends approach children routinely to pose for pictures.

In this selfie-laden world, model discretion yourself—in person and online. Handle yourself, your image, and the images of your children with respect and modesty. You protect your child from their own and others' poor judgment when you limit their access to cameras and the internet.

EVALUATE EVERY DEVICE, GAME, AND APP

Online risks are unavoidable, even with incredible monitoring software. So, if our children have devices, how do we ensure their safety?

Evaluate each application in full, one by one—as you would if signing them up for a team. Read comments, watch videos, and survey reviews before allowing the download. If you choose to authorize chatroom use, encourage the child to chat only with children they already know in person—through school, neighborhood, activities, or family. If it's not possible to restrict chat to known, safe people, look for the ability to lock chat room access within the game. If an app doesn't allow such a lockdown, it is not a safe app for children.

Help your child create a profile name and photo that don't contain identifying information—no real names, no addresses, no schools, no teams. Children can tell their friends what their usernames are if they want to start communicating online. Come up with your own "I am not a robot" system for when people reach out to your child online. If the person says, for example, that they're "Jimmy from Boy Scouts," have your child ask the person for some piece of information that only troop insiders would know. If they can't provide it, block the profile.

Use, check, and enforce the parental controls available on each device and application, but realize that children are plenty familiar with device settings and may be able to disable any controls you set. You may need to reinstate them periodically and set up some sort of accountability system for the child leaving them in place.

Also, a parental control set up on a device does not necessarily apply to everything on that device. Apps abide by their own settings, sometimes explicitly overriding choices you thought kept your child safe.

Evaluating every app and device will be tedious and time-consuming, but it is a necessary part of parenting in the 21st century. Just as you wouldn't give the keys of an eighteen-wheeler to 11-year-olds, you can't hand them a smartphone and hope the tech companies will somehow magically protect your child. If you are not yet savvy about apps and gadgets, find someone to help you—just as you'd find someone to help you install your car seat or teach your teenager how to drive if you didn't know how to do it well yourself.

READ ALL CONTENT

Read your child's chat content without hesitation—make it a routine that they expect. If you see signs of adult participants, document any available information such as a profile name, actual name, personal characteristics, or location. Take screen shots or photos of the conversations to aid authorities who may need to be involved. Also look during this review for any illegal activity, such as sending nude images.

Directly discuss chat features of any games, apps, and social media venues with your child. Look at the settings together and openly discuss your parental control decisions. By engaging your child in the discussion of the need for these limits, you teach them about the necessity of navigating thoughtfully through the internet.

Periodically ask your child to pull up any chat conversations for you to review. Express thanks to your child if they bring troublesome chat content to your attention themselves.

PLAY ALONG

Adults should play or watch the child play a game for a few rounds now and then. Join the app yourself and encourage other family members to take part. Take time to sit with the child and discuss the game as they play. Learn more about the app or game by asking the child questions. Parents' participation in online games creates a mutual understanding about game capabilities and the child's interests.

Whenever a child is using a device, keep all devices visible, like on a table, so all people in the room can view the game. This open viewing of devices shows a child plainly and boldly that you are paying attention to their internet use. If possible, link the device a child is using to a shared television for communal watching and family involvement.

Maintain your role as the parent to create and enforce limits, including time spent playing or chatting, where devices go in your home, and when devices must be powered off or turned in to an adult.

USE A MONITORING SOFTWARE PROGRAM

Monitoring software and hardware are a huge help for active families. From routers to filtering programs, your approach to electronic controls and monitoring will depend on your family size, device type, expense, and coverage. Software programs provide summary reports that include the device's history. Alternatively, programs exist to show you your child's keystrokes throughout the day and screenshots from your child's device.

Remember, though, that monitoring programs cannot stop your child from landing in dangerous territory; they simply inform caring adults when the child is headed there—toward a trap. Furthermore, the most-used apps, such as Snapchat, TikTok, and Instagram, prohibit several monitoring programs popular with parents. Savvy minors may also create alternative profiles to avoid parental detection. So protecting your child online takes work and resolve.

SUPERVISE ONLINE REPORTS

Monitoring software is only useful when parents read and act upon the provided information. For some families, devices in the hands of children create less parental free time, not more. With updates from monitoring programs, parents have more emails and notifications to read. This extra workload may be unrealistic for the modern family, especially when more than one child is online.

DON'T BUY THE OXYMORON OF "ONLINE PRIVACY"

Monitoring a child's online life is not a violation of their privacy. Online interactions are not a journal tucked under a mattress or a face-to-face conversation with a best friend over ice cream. The internet is a hunting ground for child sex abusers and predatory peers, and a child lacks the discretion to manage their own online behavior.

Parents' assumption that minors deserve freedom and liberty online makes predators' work easier. The internet has no privacy, and children desperately need to learn that from us. It feels solitary and safe, but it is the antithesis of both those things. Kids' juvenile choices are building a digital database about them that can affect their future—whether concerning relationships, jobs, or university admissions decisions. Everything online is grotesquely public. If a child wants privacy, buy them a journal with a lock and key.

TALK OPENLY ABOUT HOW TO SHIELD IDENTITY WHILE ONLINE

Children have little understanding of risk—especially intangible risks like online predators. They don't know not to use their real names, addresses, schools and mascots, and team affiliations unless we show them a different way to manage their online life. Explain in clear terms how your child's information online is like blowing a dandelion, with all the seeds blowing near and far. Teach them how to protect their identity online, then monitor and guide their online interactions as they develop this skill.

Help! When you find out about abuse online
- Report to local law enforcement authorities
- Cut off the predator's access to your child, even if this limits or suspends your child's online presence
- Keep every scrap of proof of communication—including text messages
- Take screen shots of any discussion showing escalating connection
- Keep records if your child was contacted through their phone, received anything in the mail, or was sent money
- Ask your child what other social media pages exist, possibly under another name
- Adjust your online settings and monitoring software to tighten filters
- Notify websites, app companies, and social media platforms of abuses that happen through their products

Your Risk Reduction Checklist Online

- Evaluate the decision to give your child a phone
- Begin with a dumb phone before jumping into a smart phone
- Set parental controls
- Select and download monitoring software in addition to parental controls
- Deactivate the camera on your child's phone, using stickers or other blocking methods
- Frequently survey the phone for new apps or content

- Read and review chat content on your child's social media accounts and apps
- Supervise online activities through play or direct observation
- Review all incoming reports of your child's online activity, and act rapidly upon any signs of grooming

WITH YOUR CHILD
- Determine acceptable profile information, what to share or keep private
- Discuss online grooming and predation with your child, from peers as well as strangers
- Restrict contact groups online to only known peers and adults
- Create time limits and keep personal devices in public spaces only— never in bedrooms or bathrooms
- Take up devices at the same time every day, and never allow children devices overnight

CHAPTER 12

SCHOOLS, ACTIVITIES AND SPORTS

Schools are a model for child protection. Schools train staff about abuse and diligently look for signs of a problem—all staff realize their role in protecting children. Mandated reporters are everywhere, and children's solitude is infrequent. There are established procedures for reporting questionable behaviors, and teachers and students follow a posted daily schedule with limited unstructured time. Activities and sports programs would benefit from imitating this example.

Despite all this effort invested in prevention, abuse can happen anywhere children go. Limited adult supervision in bathrooms, buses, sports complexes, and empty rooms makes for higher-risk zones for abuse than classrooms filled with many students. And, sadly, there may be predators among the teachers and staff. Their grooming behaviors, however, can be detected by attentive adults and observant students.

Schools may sometimes close ranks to protect a predatory adult, just like we see in family systems. When you report abuses to school officials, always involve law enforcement and protective agencies.

Risk Factors Rooted in Activities, Hobbies, and Extracurriculars

Extracurricular activities are not school or home. There may be no teachers or parents. Staff or volunteers become more like mentors or cool guides for the children involved. This friendly foundation for adult-child interactions can be exploited by predators moving through the stages of grooming.

Leaders of extracurricular activities, however, are well-positioned to sniff out predators. Caring adults working with children need to stay on alert for outlying adult behavior, along with other children's actions. Preying minors use after school or activities to exploit less popular or powerful kids.

RISK FACTOR 1: NO PARENTS PRESENT

Unsupervised or less-supervised youth activities like meetings and field trips are ripe for predatory adults. Most families seek out programs because childcare and positive experiences are provided for their child, but the lack of parental supervision is a built-in risk factor.

RISK FACTOR 2: RELIANCE ON VOLUNTEERS

Extracurricular activities rely heavily on unpaid volunteers, who are widely sought after and encouraged to serve in a variety of positions. This allows a predatory adult with free time or a flexible work schedule to "come to the rescue" of an organization that provides services to children. Perceived as kind and eager, a predatory adult may be handed access to children on a silver platter. If predatory adults have school-aged children, they may automatically be viewed as safe adults by virtue of having kids in the school or program.

RISK FACTOR 3: INCONSISTENT SCREENING

Volunteer screening varies widely among agencies providing youth activities. Some require a background check and references, while others require no paperwork at all and make no attempt to screen volunteers. Families are not always aware of these disparities and may assume that programs thoroughly assess all incoming volunteers.

RISK FACTOR 4: OVERNIGHT OPPORTUNITIES

Children participating in sports and hobbies experience unique overnight opportunities. Whether at conferences, camps, or travel tournaments, overnight trips serve predatory adults during all stages of grooming. Sleeping arrangements can be flexible or rearranged spontaneously. Decisions can get made on the fly by the adults present, who may not always uphold the policies. Heavily influenced by logistics, including facility layout, security concerns, and the ratio of children to adults, an adult may suggest sleeping in the room with a certain child or group of children. This offer of support is perceived positively by the other adults, who prefer not to sleep near the children. No matter what the arrangements are, children and adults co-sleeping is to be avoided for the protection of the adults and the minors.

Risk Factor 5: Unpredictable Routine

Extracurricular activities are less structured than the average school day. Children are offered flexibility in how they spend their time, resulting in opportunities for predation. For example, an extracurricular activity at a school after hours enables a predatory volunteer to explore unused unlocked spaces with an unsupervised participant.

Risk Factor 6: Staff-to-Student Ratio

Proper monitoring of students and staff hinges greatly on group size. An activity that is looking to optimize costs may admit a larger number of students than staff can adequately supervise. This sets up situations where staff may not be capable of observing questionable behavior between staff and students. The size of the group of students and number of staff should be strongly considered when you select a program for your child.

Coaches and Sport Professionals

A nine-year-old boy was chosen by his basketball coach for free coaching one on one to develop his natural ability. The coach hosted the boy at his neighborhood basketball court and invited him to stay overnight when lessons ran late. The coach's wife noticed the bed would be empty for hours during these sleepovers. She took to sleeping in front of their bedroom door to prevent him leaving. The boy's mother became suspicious after watching the coach interact with her child during a game. She was about to report the behavior when the coach introduced her to the scout for a prestigious school with a strong athletics program.

Risk Factors Rooted in Sports Teams and Athletic Clubs

Youth involvement in competitive and club league sports is a long-standing staple of a well-rounded childhood. With hundreds of thousands of children registering for youth sports around the nation, parents must be knowledgeable of the risks presented by trainers, coaches, volunteers, and staff surrounding sports. This chapter highlights how sports staff groom through coaching tasks. I will discuss the ways in which coaching provides unique access to children and why families tolerate behavioral infractions, permitting chronic predators to ransack youth sports.

You will also learn how caring coaches can protect children. Conscientious coaches must assist parents and guardians in raising the standards for behavior of all adults who encounter minor athletes. And parents who respond to disturbing behaviors have the power to affect change for the team, the league, and the community.

RISK FACTOR 1: PARENTS WANT THE EXPERIENCE TOO

Youth sports are meaningful to families—sometimes because participation is a torch carried by a parent. Memories of watching a sport or playing it as a child motivate parents to encourage their children to participate. This nostalgia can place a burden on children to succeed in a sport so they don't disappoint their parents. Parents should avoid placing high-stakes value on sports participation.

RISK FACTOR 2: TOUCHING IS PART OF THE JOB

The risk of a predator using his access as a coach or member of the sporting staff to abuse minor children is obvious. Coaches and sports professionals can be given tremendous liberty with minors' bodies. The job typically calls for touching, body positioning, staring, and physical closeness in a venue that can be either public or secluded. In the case of a personal trainer, massage therapist, or sports physician, sessions may be held in a completely private space.

Touch is widely accepted in traditional sports. The classic example is the coach who slaps the rear ends of the players as they enter or exit the field to express appreciation of their efforts. This action is public and viewed by an audience, and we may have seen it and not given it a second thought. It doesn't make butt slapping acceptable, but it does normalize, for athletes and their parents, touch initiated by the coach. While many would not consider a slap on the bottom predatory behavior, they might think differently if the coach is found to have a collection of child pornography on their computer.

If your child is in youth sports, ask questions about touch and safety. If the answers are not satisfactory, it may be time to look for another eam or organization.

As a community member and caring adult, you help shape your local youth sports with your expectations and your questions: How are children spoken to, touched, and managed by adults in this community? What are acceptable behaviors and gestures toward children on and off the field? How can I shape our youth teams to be safer places for children and adults?

As a community of child protectors, we not only need to ask ourselves what standards are acceptable, but also raise the current standard. Any adult working with young athletes should be able to perform sporting-related touches in public settings, with onlookers.

RISK FACTOR 3: INCONSISTENT STAFF TRAINING

As youth activities try to curb sexual misconduct by adults, they may purchase or adopt anti-abuse training programs that are marketed to teams and leagues. Such policies are noble: Minimize the number of predators hired. Inform volunteers about child sexual abuse and how to watch for its signs among their players. Review federal and local reporting requirements.

Unfortunately, The Aspen Institute's report on staff training norms reveals that less than one-third of youth coaches are trained in competencies required for the job of coaching, such as safety and sport instruction.[xlix] If less than one third of coaches have basic coaching training, an added requirement for training in sex abuse prevention seems unrealistic, unattainable, and, most importantly, unenforceable. This lack of training presents risk for the children involved in the program.

RISK FACTOR 4: RESPECT FOR LEADERSHIP, TRADITION, AND TRACK
RECORD

In sports culture, respect and tradition are highly valued. Youth sports
leadership relies on the reports of minors, minors' families, and other staff
to alert regional and national leaders to an issue of abuse. Fellow coaches
may struggle to notice and respond to disturbing behaviors, and they may
offer the benefit of the doubt to a fellow sports professional as a sign of
respect, especially if they have a prestigious track record.

RISK FACTOR 5: NO EDUCATION FOR KIDS

There is no mandatory or standard training for young athletes, from pre-
kindergarten through college, about recognizing sexual abuse perpetrated
by coaches and sports staff. Without such a mandate, the onus of
responsibility falls on parents and caring adults to educate and set, or
raise, standards for staff in youth sports in their community.

RISK FACTOR 6: MALE-DOMINATED PROFESSION

Most sporting professionals are not predators. Most coaches are caring
adults. Most coaches of youth sports are also male, no matter the gender
of the athletes they're coaching. According to The Aspen Institute, only
28% of coaches are female.[i] And as you know from the earlier chapters of
this book, statistics tell us that child sexual predators are overwhelmingly
male. Men working closely with a specific gender of a certain age is
standard protocol for predators, and predatory coaches blend in nicely
with the caring adults on the sidelines and in the locker rooms.

RISK FACTOR 7: FATHER FIGURE, COUNSELOR, OR DEITY

Parents seeking an adult mentor for their child look to sports for available
caring adults. These parents, who may have limited time to observe coaching, trust the adult with their child. A child is more at risk for abuse if family
supports are spotty, and sports-oriented camaraderie provides a predatory adult the opportunity to shower a child with affection and attention.

In addition to acting as a fill-in dad or counselor, cherished coaches may
take on a godlike status among their athletes—or even among parents.
When a coach is perceived as higher than humanity itself, a child will
comply with his any instruction, chore, or demand. No one is capable of
intervening or even speaking ill of such a coach, which is a predator's

dream. This is why all parents with young athletes must keep their view of any coaching staff grounded in reality. Be objective about the coach and their abilities, and retain your role as parent and authority in your child's life. Don't send your child to live with a coach or permit the coach to have the primary relationship with your child.

RISK FACTOR 8: FINANCIAL DREAMS

Sports dangle the slim promise of a path out of poverty—a possibility that millions of parents overestimate. Physical talent on the field can earn select athletes financial support through professional team contracts, university scholarships, or financial aid packages to elite prep schools. The hope for this outcome motivates families to invest heavily in the world of competitive sports. Families investing financially for financial reward are at an increased risk of predation.

Predatory coaches thrive in an environment of wishful parents. A coach decides placement on the roster and frequency of play, makes referrals, writes recommendations to scouts, and picks who receives specialized attention and extra training. Children who view sports success as the ticket to escape financial insecurity are vulnerable to coaches who wield this authority over their future. They learn to blindly trust the coach, staff, and other sports professionals.

RISK FACTOR 9: MONEY MATTERS

Affluent families invest heavily in youth sports, while families who are less well-off struggle with the ballooning expenses.[li] Financial obligations for sports participation include gear, registration fees, uniforms, extra individual coaching, and travel expenses for the child and family. This dynamic puts families at both ends of the economic spectrum at risk for predation from coaches.

Intense commitment and investment in one sport over a long period of time pushes parents to defer to coaches and keep their children involved. Parents want their child to succeed, and the coach is the means to achieve that success. Parents will say things like, "Do what coach tells you, and don't complain if it hurts. Coach knows best."

Lower-income families are vulnerable to gifts from predatory coaches because the very ability to participate in the sport is dependent on freebies or favors. The disparity within youth sports for the haves and have nots is widening greatly, especially post pandemic. Predatory coaches working with financially insecure athletes are poised to entrap a driven family set for sports achievement. For some youth athletes, the sport is their path towards future success and academic opportunities.

RISK FACTOR 10: EXTENDED ALONE TIME

Sports participation requires a tremendous time commitment from any family. These include, but are not limited to, time for practices, time for travel to competitions, time for team building and training, and time to play the sport. In the care of coaches, children become bonded to sports staff— a role that is easily exploited by a predatory sports professional.

Extremely talented athletes may even switch to homeschooling or tutoring, move away from their parents, and commit their lives at a tender age to their sport and to an astounding amount of time spent with an elite coach. These coaches have a reputation of excellence that affords them near-godlike status, and allegations of abuse or grooming are drowned in accolades and denials.

If you have an elite athlete with opportunities for national or Olympic dreams, go with them. Never let a child move away from family to be isolated with a coaching staff or an athletic program. Claim your seat as the parents and chief guardians of your child in their journey through sports, whether that takes them to the city recreational league or the Olympic trials.

RISK FACTOR 11: DEFINITIONS VARY

As child abuse spans a wide definition, so does suspicion. How many complaints are needed before leadership acts against a predatory coach? Whose suspicion matters most: players, families, colleagues?

The Safe Sport Authorization Act of 2017 mandated all nationally governed and non-nationally governed youth sports to require child sexual abuse prevention training for all sports professionals working with minors, to extend the statute of limitations, to discourage one-on-one time for adults and minors, and to make all sports professionals mandated reporters.[lii] This federal standard of care and reporting mandate give sports teams the tools to react and report suspicions of abuse. Sports professionals, I call on you to evaluate and report every allegation of abuse, whether you believe it or not. Permitting abuse of young athletes and associating with predators inside your sport is tantamount to green lighting the abuser. The athletes and their families demand better. Show respect for your athletes and their commitment to the sport by defending them and looking after them, not by commodifying them.

Signs of a Problem

WATCHING CHILDREN CHANGE OR UNDRESS

Any adult who is changing clothes with children is a problem. Any adult who finds every chance to watch children changing for a practice or event is a problem. Undressing and showering in a public locker room space should be left to same-aged minors. No adult should observe kids undress, and showering or changing while players are showering and changing should be strictly prohibited. There is no budging on this line.

SLEEPING TOGETHER

Predatory adults use times of unconsciousness to place their hands on child victims. Any adult who wishes to sleep where the children are sleeping is a bright red flag. The adult may claim safety concerns, insisting that the children need supervision. But no adult should be permitted to sleep alone with a child or children. If an adult supervisor needs to sleep with the group of students, there should be another, unrelated, non-partner adult present. No adult's bed should be neighboring the students' beds. Adults should never share a bed with any student or enter a student's bed for any reason. (See Chapter 10, At Home, for more details about protecting sleeping children.)

CREATING ALONE TIME

A staff member or volunteer who gives children recurring alone time is a bright red flag. No child in an extracurricular activity should be singled out from the rest of the students. If special attention is needed, staff should alert parents.

If you are a staff member or volunteer observing a pattern of one-on-one time between a staff member and a child participant, confront the adult with curiosity, as you learned about in the chapters on how to stop grooming. Interrupt the individual time when you encounter the two together, encourage the child to rejoin the group, and tell the adult you are confused about why the child would be here alone. Often adult confrontations scare predatory adults. Parents who cannot attend an event rely on caring adults, like you, to notice any outlying actions of the other adults participating in sports and hobbies.

HOSTING KIDS

A coach or program leader repeatedly hosting private events in a private residence, especially with overnight opportunities, should give you concern. If you are a coach wishing to host an event, schedule it during waking hours and select a location that is not your home. If you do have an event at your home, invite all parents to attend and socialize.

TOUCHING FREQUENTLY

Sports professionals who physically express affection to players is a problem. Examples of prohibited touching include full body hugging lasting longer than normal, tickling, wrestling, stroking legs or arms, lying down with players, joining player roughhousing, pinching, or tugging at uniforms or team suits. Another form of unacceptable touch from a sports professional is prolonging hands-on instruction time beyond its necessary usefulness.

Coaches grow close to their players. But professional relationships between adult sports professionals and minor athletes don't include acts of intimate affection. Displays of affection that are unacceptable include kissing, co-sleeping, messaging privately, gift giving, hand holding, picture exchanging, and dating players.

SHOWING AROUSAL

Any sign of arousal in an adult volunteer or leader while interacting with players is a major problem that needs immediate response. An erection during coaching, skills building, or private sessions is cause for grave alarm in coaching staff, athletes, and parents alike. Never ignore a staff person touching themselves while working with children.

If you observe signs of arousal, immediately interrupt the event and remove yourself and your child. You can make up something like,

"I completely forgot I left the oven on" or "I've just received a text that I must address". Once your child is removed, you can say, "I noticed your physical response to my daughter and I will be reporting this and removing my child from your program immediately."

CONDONING HAZING

Hazing means forcing a strenuous, dangerous, or humiliating task on another person or group, and it has serious and negative consequences. No coach should ignore signs of, condone, or take part in hazing. If you are a coach looking to establish traditions and team bonding, consider healthy alternatives like ropes courses, adventure outings, and team-building facilitation.

Any team or program encouraging hazing activities among players is a sign of a sports professional working to create imbalances of power among minors. This imbalance increases the likelihood of peer-on-peer abuse.

RESTRICTING PARENTAL SUPERVISION

Attempts to limit parental observation or visitation to coaching sessions is troublesome. Training or practices that are restricted from parents' view allow predators to isolate the minor athletes and avoid necessary parental oversight.

Ensuring Safety in Schools, Activities, and Sports

Parents

ASK HOW STAFF ARE SELECTED AND EVALUATED

Agencies working with youth should have a protocol for selecting and hiring staff and volunteers working near children. Before you chose an activity for your family, ask the director or supervisor of the program how they screen their staff and volunteers.

The program handbook or policy manual should be readily available to you. If you do not find the information in the program's paperwork, speak up and request more details. If the program is unable to tell you how they screen their staff, they most likely do not have a standard policy. As a

166 DUCK DUCK GROOM

parent, this lack of routine/standard screening should prompt you to look for another organization.

If no alternative exists, push the organization to up their game and strengthen their vetting and selection process. Offer tools found in this book to begin the process.

DISCUSS PROCEDURES TO PROTECT CHILDREN DURING ACTIVITIES

Child protection procedures are a responsibility all organizations assume when hosting youth. The handbook or supervisor should describe how the program is guarding against child mistreatment. A common strategy of requiring two adults with any minors is an improvement over one adult. However, child safety in a two-adult situation depends largely on the adults who are paired, their commitment to the policy, and the relationship between the two adults.

Ask about the safety protocol among minor participants: Does one exist? How will the program address safety concerns between children? These types of questions inform you as a parent about the level of foresight in a program. These parameters are a tool for your family while assessing the organization.

Notice any physical contact between the participants and staff. Acceptable friendly touches from sports professionals include high fives, fist bumps, side hugs, and a pat on the back or shoulders. Attentiveness at early stages of grooming protects children and prevents situations requiring more gumption later.

OBSERVE THE PROGRAM AND ASK CURRENT PARTICIPANTS

Visit and observe the class or activity. Parents of current students may also be a wonderful source of information. Ask the supervisor if there is another parent who would can talk to you about their family's experience with the program. This helps you begin to build the force field community to protect children through open communication, high standards for adult behavior, and active observation.

Parents, if you see signs of favoritism or excess attention, speak up— immediately and openly—to the coach, staff, and nearby parents: "I'm curious why Coach Steve is only meeting privately with Tommy. Has anyone else noticed this pattern?" You aren't assigning blame; you are posing a question.

ATTEND ACTIVITIES

Attend events, activities, and field trips whenever possible. Your effort communicates to program staff that you have an eye on your child. If you are unable to attend regularly, consider teaming up with another parent to take turns attending and paying attention to the children from both families. This allows you the chance to build a community focused on parental support.

Another suggestion is to show up unannounced to events or meetings. The staff response to a parent's observation should be welcoming. A random appearance keeps staff on their toes and gives you an opportunity to see how the staff and children are interacting. If you can't drop in on an event, such as a field trip where students are transported by bus or facilities have limited capacity, you can observe from a distance.

INTRODUCE YOURSELF TO INSTRUCTORS AND VOLUNTEERS

Get face to face with the lead staff or volunteers of the program. Even a quick hello or thanks at the beginning and end of a session facilitate a relationship that is beneficial for you both. Having a relationship will make it easier for you to bring up any safety concern you may have. Also, it may be easier for a staff member to ask you about your child's experience with a questionable adult participant. It is extremely important to use the time at pick up, drop off, and events.

Leaders, Coaches, and Volunteers

Participation in sports is a fantastic way of teaching children teamwork, resilience, and physical fitness. You can protect minors, families, and adults, while not sacrificing love of a hobby, activity, or sport. Establishing and enforcing clear and unyielding expectations of adults is necessary to protect children's activities from predators.

ESTABLISH OPEN COMMUNICATION

For coaches and volunteers, welcome every child and their guardians at the start by communicating your commitment to a fun, safe experience.

Tell them that you are always interested in listening to their opinion about the team and team actions. "I want us to have the best year yet. I will be available to speak with you as needed and am always available if a problem comes up during the season. Parents, my door is always open. Kids, my door is always open." By taking the steps to state clearly that you prioritize athlete safety, you set the standard for the team and yourself.

ALL CONTACT IS PUBLIC AND OPEN

The youth sports industry works best when it aims to protect the safety of the child and the reputation of the adult. Coaches, let players and parents know that you will meet with them in open spaces or with doors open. Limit or completely avoid one-on-one time with minor players.

Coaches and volunteers, please send group emails and texts to all parties. For example, coaches should not text private messages to children from their personal cell phones. If a scheduling message needs to be distributed, it should be between the program staff and the adult caregiver responsible for that child. At a minimum, two adults should be included in all emails and messages.

Inform families that you will stay in public spaces after a practice for care-givers to pick players up, that you will stay near others if available, and you will never seclude a child. Hold team-sponsored events in public venues or, if you host an event in your home, invite all parents to stay and mingle.

CREATE AND UPHOLD A CULTURE OF PREVENTION

Coaches and volunteers, once you've stated your intent to listen openly, you are then responsible for setting a culture for your team. Speak to children kindly and avoid derogatory language. Model and teach good sportsmanship. These practices complement a protective youth sports culture.

Always focus on professionalism and respect while interacting with the team and the parents. Coaches are not meant to be one of the kids on the team. Buddying up with and showing favoritism to youth athletes is dangerous for coaches. Always use clean language, and never create secrets with minor athletes.

LIMIT TOUCH

To reposition a youth athlete, use your words first. Most position changes can be explained verbally. Alternatively, have a child with proper form demonstrate to the other children. If touch is still needed, begin by asking permission from the child. Make any coaching touches purposeful, brief, and public, ideally with other adults present.

ACTIVELY COMBAT HAZING RITUALS

Investigate your league's policy on hazing. If none exists, advocate to your supervisor to include a hazing deterrent.

Establish a foundation with your players that hazing is prohibited and could result in expulsion from the team. Find constructive ways to build allegiances among your players, such as ropes courses, social events in public venues, and rewards for players showing sportsmanship to teammates.

Report any hazing activities to parents, along with the consequence meted out for disrespecting the team. Always enforce policies that keep children on the team, and any adults involved, safe.

Help! When you find out about abuse in schools, activities, or sports
- Report the abuse to the police, school, program, and local and national organization immediately
- Discuss the incident openly with your child, restating your love of them and your belief of their experience
- Depending on the response, remove your child from the program, school, or activity
- If asked, you can state unacceptable conduct of staff was your reasoning for leaving. Be careful stating specific names to avoid negative legal consequences
- Find a replacement activity

Your Risk Reduction Checklist for School, Activities, and Sports

• Ask about safety policies, training practices, and hiring requirements
• Check for staff on the local and national sex offender registry
• Attend when possible or have an attentive adult fill in
• Talk to other parents with children participating
• Observe staff interactions with the children
• Restrict private sessions or meetings

WHAT PARENTS AND COMMUNITIES CAN DO

CHAPTER 13

PARENTING THAT PREPARES

In Parts 1 and 2, I described how you can fulfill your responsibility to protect your children against potential predators. (Again, it is your job, not a child's, to spot and stop any concerning behavior.)

This part takes your parenting skills one step further by explaining specific topics that children need to hear about, so that they will be prepared to recognize problem situations if they arise and have the words to talk about them with you. Let your kids in on some truths. Their risk of becoming the target for a predatory adult or peer diminishes when they recognize their power.

A skilled predator may still succeed in entrapping a child, but having some straightforward information and vocabulary will make it less likely that your child will be confused if someone tries to groom or abuse them. And always remember that a child is never at fault for the actions of a predator. Children are ignorant to the incremental and harmful escalation of adults who are grooming them. Learning to dodge grooming tricks reduces a family's risk of becoming prey.

Throughout this book, I encourage you to lead your family and children. Leadership, like grooming, is active, not passive, and caring adults need to work harder than any potential predator. Proactively communicate with your children. When your child comes to you with a question, no matter how trivial, create space to listen and address their concern. Your child is depending on you to guide them. This chapter gives every family some practical dos and don'ts for creating a family culture that makes your children too difficult and inconvenient to be worth the hassle for a predator.

Do's

TALK ABOUT CHILD SEXUAL ABUSE WITH YOUR CHILDREN

Avoiding the subject of child sexual abuse makes our children less safe. Communities that discuss child sexual abuse have fewer instances of sexual abuse. Do not describe the details of sexual abuse to your child, but instead remind them that no one is exempt from the safety measures your family follows. Keep it short and simple: "Not everyone we know wants to keep you safe, so we follow the same safety practices no matter who you're with."

TEACH YOUR CHILD HOW TO ASSERT THEMSELVES

The best way to reduce any child's risk of sexual abuse is make them too difficult to be good prey. Recognize your child's vulnerabilities and intentionally combat the risks associated with those vulnerabilities.

Teach your child how to communicate "no" to a peer or an adult through their body language, voice, volume, gestures, and eye contact. This communication draws attention, and attention dissuades potential predators. Especially in settings where you aren't there, it is valuable for your child to know how to effectively raise their voice above the room.

Children can use their bodies as protection from predation, even without training in self-defense or martial arts. For example, for a child living in a major city taking public transportation, body safety measures include sitting close to a bus driver or public transportation conductor for increased visibility, sitting near a mother with children, selecting a subway car with ample space, keeping eyes up and open to people who may be staring at them during the ride, and limiting device use when traveling alone. These little decisions make it more difficult for a predator to victimize that child.

GIVE PERMISSION TO SAY 'NO, THANKS'

Teach your child that their body belongs entirely to them and they can always say no to anyone touching them. Encourage them to remove themselves immediately from a situation that makes them uncomfortable and to tell you about any kind of touch from anyone, no matter the title or role that person holds.

Naysayers say it is disrespectful to reject physical displays of affection from close friends and family members, but a caring relationship with an adult or peer never rests upon bodily access to your child.

Children will routinely experience touch from caring adults in school, community, and family settings. These touches should occur in plain sight with no attempt to cover or obscure the contact. If an adult in your family's life makes a big deal about the lack of touch from your child, it may be a warning sign. Caring adults acknowledge your values and support your decisions. Anything else is a tip-off for you and your family.

EXPLAIN THE DIFFERENCES BETWEEN SECRECY, PRIVACY, AND SURPRISE

Children may initially struggle with these concepts. Secrecy is something to hold onto out of fear of the consequences of it being revealed. Privacy is something to be held in confidence out of respect for someone or a group of people. Surprises are keeping information, for a limited period, away from a certain person or persons for the purpose of giving them something positive, special, or celebratory.

It's important that children understand who should know what information and when. Thus, we do our children a service by clearly explaining the difference between keeping a secret, keeping private information, and receiving a surprise from someone else. It's important to also explain this language to our families and other caring adults in our children's lives.

Secrets

Predators use secrets to manipulate and dominate a child. These secrets hold the child captive, mute and fearful, and are used as a weapon against the child. "You don't want your parents to find out what you have done with me, do you? Then we need to keep it a secret." Secrets carry heavy burdens of shared guilt, and these emotions are burdensome enough for adults! Be blunt with your children about the risks and burdens of secrets. Emphasize with them that no relationship, in person or online, requires, expects, or demands secrecy.

Extended family or close friends may offer your child a special treat or a prize, saying "Let's not tell Mommy and Daddy about this ice cream sundae. It'll be our little secret." This seems harmless, but tiny secrets lay the foundation for larger and larger secrets over the course of a relationship with a predator. Educate your family members, close friends, and other key adults that secrets are prohibited—that the use of the word "secret" is problematic and your child has been educated to immediately tell a safe caring adult if anyone asks them to keep something secret. Beware adults who ridicule your rules about secret-keeping. Establishing a secrecy-free zone helps your child maneuver through the world at school and in the community at large.

Privacy

Medical or mental health status, financial status, legal status, and personal issues are private. How much money is in your bank account? Private. How much do you weigh? Private. What happened at the meeting with your principal? Private. Your report card results? Private.

Privacy conveys information within a small or medium-sized group that is held in confidence due to the sensitivity of the information. For example, the location of a hidden house key is private. It is easy to tell the child that the key's location should only be known by people who may need to enter the house. Would this information be suitable for their social media page? School announcements? Billboards along the interstate? No. While this information is not secret, because it is known by several people, it is private and should not be shared outside that designated group.

Personal information about themselves or other relatives is also private. The location of a birthmark, the status of a pregnancy, and the results of a blood test are examples of family matters that are private.

We often tell children, incorrectly, that their body parts covered by swimsuits are private and are not to be shared with others. Children should instead be taught that their bodies, in their entirety, are private. For example: If you're wearing a hat, it is viewable by all. If a friend or family member approached you and touched, adjusted or removed your hat, you might think it odd and out of sorts. Your hat is not hidden or "private," yet you still feel it is yours to wear as you wish.

The benefits to teaching children that the body they live in is private are multifold and establish for your child a sense of ownership and empowerment. It also teaches them that touch anywhere on their body can be unwanted or confusing, not just genital touch. Thus they can speak up and out against any type of touch from anyone. Predators will engage in playful, casual touching to familiarize a child with the feel of their hands on their body and to desensitize them to physical touch. But a child who knows that their whole body is private is equipped to let people know if a peer or adult touches them in any way that is peculiar or intimate.

Surprises

Surprises are an important ingredient of magic-making during childhood, and they should not be banned or limited for children or within families. Surprises always get shared, accompanied by presents, magical creatures (Tooth Fairy, elves, Santa Claus, leprechauns), or unique experiences. Once a child realizes that a surprise is about honoring and celebrating another person, they understand that a surprise cannot be effectively used by a predator.

DECLARE WHERE YOU STAND

We must clearly and frequently voice our expectations for touch and intimacy so that any unwanted behaviors can be recognized and quickly addressed. Children without guideposts are at increased risk for their ignorance to be used against them. Children with no understanding of how and why an adult or peer should have physical contact with them are vulnerable to the predators in their midst.

If we are silent about our values and expectations around sex and intimacy, children will concoct their own answers from friends, other influences, and the internet. And they will be at greater risk from predatory adults and peers because we have failed to outline the conduct that is out of place. Speak up often about what you believe and why you believe it, and do not be put off by an eye roll, an "oh, Mom," or other shrugs or comebacks from your child. Children want to hear your opinion; their ears are open and receiving our signals.

CREATE A FAMILY PRIVACY PROTOCOL

As the adult in the home, set expectations of behavior. The rules of engagement for playing outside might include asking for permission, saying where you are going, putting on shoes, and staying out of the street. Similarly, establish a personalized privacy protocol—a straightforward code of conduct to protect children and adults.

The specifics are up to you, but they should reflect your respect for your privacy and your children. For example: bedroom doors stay open with company in the house, everyone must knock before entering a bedroom, and bathroom doors remain closed during bathing and toileting. This simple set of protocols, agreed upon by all household members, establishes your norm. As your child ventures into other homes for activities or friendships, their behavior should follow their own family's protocol of respect and privacy, even if the rules at their friend's house differ.

PRACTICE DIFFICULT SCENARIOS

Practicing a difficult skill with a safe parent is a fabulous tool that is always at your fingertips, so role-play common scenarios with your child. For example, discuss a situation where your child needs to change clothes privately for an activity. You can suggest using a bathroom stall to change, because that is likely the most private space. Alternatively, find a time to change before the activity, like right after school or class. If a private space is not available, turn away from the group of peers or adult observers to change. In a worst-case scenario, refuse to change and sit out. Remind your child that you need to know if anyone watches them undress, whether it's an adult or a peer.

SPEAK UP

As soon as you are aware of grooming behaviors by an adult in your child's life, contact that adult immediately to request a meeting, or even drop by their physical office space unannounced. If the meeting is in person, keep the door open and go when you know other staff will be present. Avoid early mornings, lunch breaks, and evenings.

Don't allow the adult to shuffle you inside and close the door. Stand at the open doorway, speak confidently, and politely say something like: "I saw that you'd texted my daughter asking for a picture in her cheer costume. I appreciate your supporting her cheerleading, but do not text my daughter without including me on the message. I know you well, and I wanted to tell you in person that our family does not condone adolescent picture sharing. Asking for pictures is not professional and could be misinterpreted." The adult will typically retreat and assure you that their communication was only intended to support the child. But now this adult is on notice, and you've handled it in a public and polite manner.

Furthermore, the surrounding staff have heard the conversation in its entirety. This is crucial because the secrecy and silence of coworkers, friends, and family allows predators to perpetuate abuse.

PLAY THE MATCHING GAME

When our children have a clear idea of safe behaviors, it helps clarify behaviors by people that are out of place with their roles. Like a matching game, certain behaviors come with adult roles: A mother can tuck a child into bed at nighttime, but a coach should not tuck in a child. These small examples illuminate the mismatch to your child. Below is a list of casual and intimate physical contacts for you to review with your child and talk about which acts are fitting with which adults in their life.
• Shoulder touch
• Fist bump, high five, other hand gestures
• Handshake
• Side hug
• Full frontal contact hug
• Knee touch
• Arm around the waist or hip
• Holding hands
• Kissing on the cheek
• Kissing on the lips
• Kissing on the face
• Tickling
• Wrestling
• Bathing
• Bathroom assistance
• Butt tap or smack
• Massage
• Tucking in or bedtime routine
• Co-sleeping or bedsharing
• Genital wiping or cleaning
• Dressing assistance

On a basic level, adults' actions should match their roles in a child's life. Our obligation is to prepare our children to identify the mismatches, even when we are not with them. This lowers their risk for sexual abuse.

EXPLORE THE WHO, WHAT, WHERE, WHEN, HOW, AND WHY

One way we can reduce the risk of our children being preyed upon is to explain that the same touch can be healthy or harmful, depending on who, what, where, and why it's happening. The context is the key to understanding the "fit," or lack thereof.

Holding hands, for example, can be a harmless touch; however, the situation of handholding affects its significance. A teacher holding your child's hand as they cross a busy intersection on a field trip seems like a condonable touch—she is reflexively grabbing the child's hand for their safety and protection. A teacher holding your child's hand under her desk and against her lap, however, is a disturbing touch.

It's all just holding hands—there are no clothes removed and no private parts involved, but your adult awareness of the context interprets one touch as necessary for safety and the other as ill fitting. It's important that we share these distinctions with our children. See the Appendix for more information on using this tool.

USE PROPER NAMES FOR BODY PARTS

Many mothers and fathers shy away from openly discussing bodies, genital functions, sex, and self-touch with their children. The common practice of using pet or nonsense names for private parts is a glaring example of this parental dilemma, and it can create misunderstanding for a child who's been victimized.

Any made-up words for the body make it difficult for your child to relay a story of predation. If your daughter calls her vagina a pocketbook, she is helpless if asked specific questions about an event involving her genitals or someone else's. A playful term for the genital area conveys silliness, instead of respect, and predators can use the pet names to equate their abusive touching to a game.

Teach your child the medical terms for their private parts and those of the other sex. Use those words in your home and, when suitable, in public—like at the doctor's office. Children pick up on your attitudes toward the body, intimacy, and development. Show your child your comfort and confidence by respecting and using the proper labels. Below is a list of seven terms for you to review.

1. Breasts and nipples: the glands that provide human milk to new babies. All people have breasts, but only people with female hormone post puberty can breastfeed babies
2. Buttocks/Butt: the muscle that protects your backside and anus
3. Anus: the opening where poop exits the body, protected by the buttock
4. Penis: the external male genitals, also where urine exits the body
5. Testicles: the two round nodules under the penis where sperm is produced and stored
6. Vulva: the external female genitals
7. Vagina: the internal genital structure of people born female

It is easy to educate children through the typical acts of hygiene. The bathroom is an opportunity to specify which parts of the body are doing what action. For example, a little boy learning to use the toilet should be educated that his penis is where urine exits the body. The anus is where poop exits the body. Little boys will experience the periodic hardening of their genitals. Simply explain to them that every now and again the penis fills with blood and becomes hard. This will allay fears they may have as well as prevent them from approaching someone else for information. These conversations should never convey disgust, secrecy, or shame. They should instead create a venue for healthy self-exploration and biological understanding.

ACKNOWLEDGE SELF-TOUCH

Children explore their genitals, just as adults do, because it is pleasurable. Self-touch is normal and, within reason, should be respected. As a responsible caregiver, it is important to educate your child about the times, places, and ways they can self-explore.

For example, if you notice your son or daughter touching themselves repeatedly, simply make eye contact and gently remind the child of their options: They can go to a private space where they are permitted to touch themselves or they can stay where they are and stop touching themselves. Be explicit about where they can engage in that behavior. Possible options may include in the bathroom alone with the door closed, in bed alone, or in another solitary space away from others and onlookers.

Since predators will test a child by watching them without touching them, or by asking a child to watch while they touch themselves, it is important to stress that any acts of self-touch should be done without any observers or company, no matter the onlooker's age, role or title.

Allow your child time to be by themselves. Autonomy to explore and feel in control of their own body is an integral component to helping them develop self-acceptance. Around the age of four or five, children become more aware of the idea of privacy. Teach and model the importance of modesty and having privacy for personal care. When you are showering, using the toilet, engaging in sexual intimacy with a partner, or tending to acts of hygiene, close the door and use door locks to illustrate personal respect.

Remember your goal as a parent is to raise healthy children who are comfortable in their own skin and will one day have sexual health—including enjoying touch from someone they love. A child who learns to take care of their body through hygiene, sleep, and tenderness is more capable of advocating for themselves than a child without any skills in understanding their bodies.

PRACTICE THE SKILLS

Knowing ways to prevent, respond to, and report sexual abuse is part of developing independence and self-reliance. Give kids the opportunities to practice street-smart skills in familiar public settings—the grocery store, barbershop, neighborhood markets. With you in sight, the actual risks are limited, and the benefits are enormous. For example, before you go to the grocery store, sit in the car and talk about how to handle situations that may occur through the aisles. How do you respond to a blocked aisle? What if someone bumps into your cart? How do you respond if someone begins a conversation with you? How much should we tell strangers about ourselves? Discuss your goal for the shop, including why you've picked this store and this time of day to shop. Run the tape all the way through in your conversation, evaluating potential risks: Positive ending? A successful shop ends with everyone behaving inside the store, purchasing what is needed, and returning to the car in a timely manner. Negative ending? We return to the car without the necessary items and we spent longer than expected. Although this may sound trivial, your everyday decision-making models to your child about how self-protection is woven into your thinking. Your goal is to decrease their ignorance with the purpose of properly preparing them.

You may decide to have your child learn some basic self-defense techniques, or even a form of martial arts such as karate or taekwondo, to have knowledge of physical techniques to combat an immediate threat.

EXPAND THE TOOLKIT

Contrary to popular belief, cell phones don't eliminate risks. Phones may be out of power or signal range—or a predator may confiscate them. Children need more tools at their disposal than making a phone call to you or taking a picture. They need to be educated in common-sense safety behaviors. Behaviors such as covering school logos when in public, withholding personal details, avoiding mood altering substances, identifying safe adults in a given location, and paying attention to their surroundings, including people or cars that may be following them.

Don'ts

DON'T TRAIN KIDS TO BE PASSIVE

We teach kids to say yes, to do as they are told, to avoid questioning authority figures, and not to act disruptively. These skills of cooperation, while necessary and respectful, can paralyze a child who needs to protect themselves against a predatory adult.

Practice what to say, how loud to say it, and what tone of voice when handling a testing adult or peer. For example, if an adult makes an odd or sexual joke with them, teach them to ask direct questions—"Why are you telling me this?—or to respond with humor: "You must have me confused with someone who thinks that's funny." Teach your child to repeat exactly what the adult or peer has said in a volume three times as loud with a confused facial expression. This will attract attention and attention is usually the last thing a predator wants to receive from safe adults. Alternatively, a child can loudly say, "Did you just say (repeat what was said) to me?" This type of honest communication training helps your child deal with the moment in the moment, avoiding the awkwardness of handling a situation after it's passed. Adults can use these techniques as well to handle strange adult encounters.

DON'T ASSUME ABUSE INVOLVES ONLY GENITALS

People commonly—and erroneously—assume that all child sexual abuse involves sexual organs. It is crucial that we all understand that adult interactions with our children can be abusive without involving any private parts.

Not every adult in contact with your child should have physical access or offer physical affection. Your child needs to learn from you about when certain kinds of touch may be necessary (medical setting), wanted (grandparent or girlfriend), or expected (sports settings). Take the guesswork out of what kind of touch they can expect and what kind of touch is appropriate. We prepare our children by having these discussions frequently, casually, and clearly.

A vital part of these lessons needs to be the "fit" of touching within a relationship—whether it is in place or out of place for the people involved, depending upon their history with the child and their roles in their lives. Out of place behaviors, even if they aren't sexual, are red flags. It's our job to notice them as potential grooming activities and intervene before another child falls victim to sexual abuse.

DON'T BE NAKED

Prohibit adult nudity with children. Keep yourself dressed around minors, and demand that other adults be fully clothed. There is no reason for a child to ever see a non-family adult naked.

Consider the age of your children and their development when deciding how to handle nudity in your home. For example, a mother with a 12-year-old son should not move about the house undressed, even though family nudity may have been casual when the boy was three.

Remember that what your child experiences in your home becomes normal to them, and a predator will exploit a child's comfort with naked adults. Don't let that be your child. Save nakedness for the bathroom and bedroom, without company.

DON'T USE "GOOD TOUCH, BAD TOUCH"

Well-intended adults often tell children that touch comes in two categories: good touch and bad touch. The problem is that touch is neither all good nor all bad. A hug from the wrong person is a bad touch. A genital touch by a nurse inserting a catheter before a medical procedure is, though awkward, a good touch.

Caring adults need to remember that predators exploit a child's physical comforts repeatedly in minuscule ways. If a child thinks all non-private-part touching fits in the "good" touch category, then predatory adults can more easily manipulate the child through touching hands, shoulders, chests, or legs. These seemingly "good" touches escalate until genital touch is the next frontier.

If a child is taught that all touch that avoids their private areas is safe, then they are less likely to talk to caring adults about incidents of touching that may be part of a predator's progression toward abuse. Teach your child that their whole body is private and that they don't have to accept any touch anywhere.

DON'T FORCE TOUCH

There is no pressing reason for a non-parental adult to touch a child, unless it is for immediate safety. Most touch should be child-initiated, meaning that a caring adult should make themselves open to physical touch from a child but not force touch upon them.

We have all seen or heard the shift away from mandated physical affection ("Go hug your grandma") and toward teaching children to initiate touch they wish at the time—including no touch at all. This type of parenting prepares children to better manage interactions with peers and adults outside of our company.

If you have typically demanded that your child offer physical touch, consider shifting gears to place more value on eye contact, manners, and vocal expressions to interact with people. Let your family and friends know that they can ask for physical affection from the child, but that your children are free to choose the level of affection for themselves.

DON'T TELL KIDS, "IF TOUCH MAKES YOU FEEL…"

Parents and educators tell children to notify a caring adult or parent if someone's touch makes them feel bad. Unfortunately, this phrase makes two assumptions: that abuse feels bad and that children recognize abuse as abuse. Neither of these is true all the time.

If a child thinks positively of a predator, the child may interpret abusive actions as a show of love, not harm, and affection feels good—even when coming from an abusive peer or adult. These bewildering internal and external messages overwhelm child sexual abuse victims, increasing their unearned shame. When a child's body responds with signs of sexual arousal, that shame and confusion grows.

Child abuse survivors struggle to pinpoint actions against them as abuse because predators are skilled con artists. Children need adults to recognize abuse as abuse.

DON'T SAY "UNCOMFORTABLE"; REPLACE WITH A BODY RESPONSE

Stop using the word "uncomfortable" in connection with people's relationship with your child. It tells us nothing. A seat is uncomfortable. A hot room is uncomfortable. People are not uncomfortable.

Lead your child to better describe their experiences using signals their bodies may give them. These body signals may include:
• Racing heart
• Sweating hands
• Red face, flush
• Laughing or smiling nervously
• Tummy pain like you want to throw up
• Feeling of needing to poop
• Feeling hot all over
• Wanting to leave or escape the situation
• Shaky knees, difficulty standing
• Shortness of breath
• Difficulty thinking or speaking clearly
• Body tightness or tenseness

Offer kids the chance to sit with you and talk about what body signals they experience and when. Ask them to describe how their body feels when you are together. The child might use words like warm, safe, protected, happy, comfortable, at home, and able to breathe. Then ask them to describe how their body felt during a recent event that you know made them "uncomfortable." You may hear words that are on the list above. This guided experience with a safe adult can be done quickly and easily, and it is invaluable in helping children learn to pay attention to their internal signs. Explore and talk about how our body sends us clues about our emotions. This serves them—and their safety—throughout childhood. Plus it is a good reminder for us as adults to listen to our bodies as we interact with adults and peers of our children. They may be trying to tell us something.

The Message

How you educate your children shapes their ability to protect themselves. Adults unwittingly expose their children to harm by avoiding the topics they fear. Do not give in to the desire to turn your eyes away and bury your head in the sand.

Simple conversations about tough topics give children the tools to explain any situation that may arise, whether in childish play between young children or an abusive offense from a predator. They can better communicate the details of an incident if they know specific terms for the parts of their bodies.

The children growing up in households with open communication about sexual abuse are more protected than children whose parents never talk about it. Your child's safety education lies in your hands. No one else will work as diligently to protect your child as you.

CHAPTER 14

CREATING FORCE FIELD COMMUNITIES

This chapter sheds light on ways all communities can build force fields of protection around their children. The safest communities weave multiple defense strategies together. If you live in this type of community, congratulations! This section should be a refresher in the ways you are protecting your spaces while offering you some new pointers. If you long for a safer community, recruit like-minded parents to review this material and form groups to implement these recommendations anywhere children go. Let's get practical about how protective policies make adults and children safer.

Best Practices for Community Safety

Communities that prioritize child safety construct protections through their policies, facilities, staff, and communication. Each segment offers a guard post for children. Check the following sections against your community activities and spaces. If you notice room for improvement, share these ideas with supervisors and leaders to encourage them to boost their child safety measures.

POLICIES

Policies are the official rules of behavior of a given company or organization. Even though they are written down, they are not intended to be static. Review and update policies twice a year using input from parents and lived experience of staff to craft more effective, relevant policies.

Policies might include requirements for training or professional development. These requirements ensure that the organization has a baseline of understanding about child sex abuse prevention, and they prevent staff from blaming any staff members' poor or criminal behavior on lack of knowledge. Companies can do things like sponsor an expert speaker or continuing education opportunities.

Policies can also lay out ironclad rules about supervision of children: Establish a fixed staff-to-student ratio and implement a two-adult policy. If two trained, educated staff members are working together with a group of children, the risk that a child will be abused plummets.

Policies are incomplete if they don't address enforcement and organizational hierarchy. Having a required procedure for reporting questionable or abusive behavior removes any personal decision-making by an involved adult who sees something concerning. And policies only have value if they are followed, so every community needs a hierarchy of enforcement.

FACILITIES

All facilities that children routinely attend should emphasize visibility whenever possible. Encourage public meetings in large gathering halls. If your space is a room, open the blinds, swing doors wide open, and keep the lights on. When doors must be closed for safety purposes, ensure that the room is visible through windows on the door or open windows. The more visibility there is into a room with children and adults, the greater safety for children and adults.

Unused spaces should remain locked. I recommend having a master key at a central office desk, requiring a sign out with a date and time. Facilities where all staff and volunteers have individual keys are more difficult to safeguard—especially when multiple groups use the space.

For added safety, develop a sign in/sign out process for staff, volunteers, and visitors. This is a useful reference in the event of a safety concern. The records should be stored for several months.

All facilities should be welcoming to parents and guardians when their children are present. This open-door policy creates partners out of parents, and parents should be given a copy of building access and use policy during their enrollment or admission process.

STAFF

Any staff members working alongside children inside your organization need a thorough evaluation. A proper assessment always includes the following:
- Name and address verification—including alias or potential different names
- Social Security number
- Education verification
- Employment history verification
- Reference verification
- Background check—local, state, and national (international if applicable)
- Drug test
- Sex offender registry check

Organizations must determine what prior criminal charges or convictions disqualify someone from volunteering or being hired. I recommend not engaging individuals with child endangerment, domestic violence, or assault convictions.

Always contact references and ask if the applicant would still be eligible to work at their previous company. While employment laws may prohibit businesses from describing a former employee's behavior, a former employer would be allowed to say "this candidate would be ineligible to work here."

For in-person interviews, develop real-world questions with open-ended language. For example, "How would you handle a child who tells you they want to share a secret with you?" If applicants have to respond with more than "yes" or "no," you get a better idea about their fit for a role in your organization.

Once someone is brought on board, they should go through an orientation and training process. This should include, at a minimum, job training, professional development, facilities safety policies, child abuse and neglect education, and reporting requirements for your organization.

In addition to providing all staff with your organization's child sex abuse reporting policies and procedures, post the local, state, and national reporting hotline information in a common area. This encourages staff to freely report allegations of abuse. People who report abuse allegations are protected by law, assuming the reporting was not fabricated.

Staff members should undergo annual performance evaluations that incorporate supervisory feedback and parents' comments and experience. This information can be collected through in-person questions, email surveys, or even a comment card drop box in a public area. Review this feedback for patterns, issues, or accolades to share with staff members.

COMMUNICATION

Welcome every participant and begin every program with a copy of your organization's policies. Policies should include how and when to report allegations of abuse and to whom.

Foster communication with parents by regularly circulating updates, infor-mation, and requests for critiques and feedback within your community. A good time to seek input is within the first month, at the midway point, and before the program concludes. Take all comments seriously, and follow up as needed directly with the adults who provided feedback.

Provide opportunities for guardians to interact with staff members by including family members in on-site events and celebrations. Within a community, transparency benefits your program and leadership. If any safety breach occurs, immediately inform all guardians (while not providing identifying information about the child or staff). Any attempt to ignore or cover up allegations against staff harms the perception of the program. Respect your participants enough to share pertinent information in a timely manner.

Create a Community of Mandated Reporters

A mandated reporter is someone legally required to contact authorities within a specified amount of time if abuse is suspected or confirmed. Examples of mandated reporters include mental health workers, school staff, medical professionals, clergy, law enforcement, and childcare workers. Mandated reporter laws differ from state to state, but there are always legal consequences if a mandated reporter fails to notify proper authorities.

Even if you are not a mandated reporter, notify proper agencies if you suspect child abuse. Anyone can report abuse to police or child protective agencies, and the reporting is anonymous. If all adults acted like mandated reporters, fewer children would need to rely on their own courage to stop a domineering adult or peer. Since convicted child predators rarely have only one victim, the start of an investigation can set the ripple of change in motion that is needed to prevent further abuse.

Support the Vulnerable Kids

Predators look for children who are missing something, such as stability, affection, love, peace, or emotional support. And unhappy children actively seek out any loving, willing, and seemingly helpful adult or peer. Vulnerable children run headlong into the lion's den without the slightest understanding of a potential predator's desire or intent. These kids require attentive adults like you to watch out for them and do something. Caretaking communities offer the perfect wrap around to struggling families.

Parents and Guardians

There is nothing powerful about targeting children. Predators aren't big and bad. They're pathetic, and they pick on the weakest members of society. They may be everywhere, but they are outnumbered by attentive caring adults like you.

DOCUMENT PATTERNS OF PREDATION

Reporting is a crucial piece of the larger equation to ousting a predator that is roaming your community. Caring adults may feel trapped by the limitations of a justice system that relies on proof and evidence. Document all strange or outlying behaviors involving a potential predator. Build a case through your observations, including screen shots, phone records, and any other proof you have.

According to the National Incidence Study of Child Abuse and Neglect, about 55 percent of all reported cases are investigated by child protective agencies.[liii] The rest are screened out for a lack of adequate information. That means almost half of ALL reported cases aren't even investigated.

REPORT ABUSE TO POLICE YOURSELF

Follow the same protocol for every suspicion of abuse, no matter the child or alleged perpetrator. Remember, you are not the investigator, judge, or jury. You are simply alerting the agencies to do their job. Reporting does not guarantee an arrest or a protective outcome for a child, but reporting potential abuse is crucial to stopping a predator.

Anyone discouraging you from acting to stop a suspected sexual predator is as dangerous as the predator. Don't listen to people who tell you they'll take care of the reporting and you should keep quiet. No one watches out for your child like you.

NOTIFY THE SUPERVISOR

As a caring adult, reach out to any program director, supervisor, or employer to share your experience with the predator. Schedule an in-person meeting, without the predator present, and bring any proof of escalating abusive behavior. If you are aware of other adults who share your concerns, invite them to attend as well. Kids should not participate.

To prepare, identify your requests before you enter a face-to-face private meeting. Do you want the person released from their job or removed from the community? Are you looking for more supervision from the organization? Are you simply alerting the company? Do you want the predator kicked off the team? Does the person you are meeting with have hiring and firing authority? Detail the concrete results or actions you expect to stem from your meeting. Groomed families experience devastating sorrow when nothing happens after an allegation of abuse.

USE MEDIA AND PUBLICITY TO PROTECT CHILDREN

If those with authority to intervene refuse to act, you may want to contact the media—especially to illuminate a possible agency-wide coverup of ongoing abuses. This is a difficult path, and you cannot control what happens to a story once you have shared it with reporters and their readers. But media coverage is often what finally works, when nothing else does, to trigger an investigation, consequences, and an end to ongoing abuse from a powerful person or organization. To be successful, this route usually requires that several families with similar allegations of abuse come forward, after the initial report to the local authorities.

COOPERATE WITH INVESTIGATIONS

Allegations of abuse spark an investigation of the report. The investigating agency contacts the child's family, but the source of the allegation stays anonymous. According to the Child Maltreatment 2020 report, protective agencies typically investigated allegations within ninety-nine hours of the initial contact.[liv] Professionals interview the victim, alleged perpetrator, and any additional witnesses. If your child is interviewed, stay with them and help them answer the questions honestly.

DON'T CONTACT THE PREDATOR

Once you've reported an allegation of abuse, do not contact the alleged perpetrator of abuse, even if you are related to, married to, or close to them. You need to act calmly, even if you are raging inside, and focus all your efforts on recovering and protecting your child's well-being. Throttling, beating up, or killing a predator will not improve the situation, and it jeopardizes the investigation, the child's future, and your own future—such that you could become unable to help anyone.

DON'T ALERT ANOTHER CHILD'S PARENT

If a child who is not your own tells you they are being abused, don't notify the parents, even though you may understandably be distraught. Your impulse to notify the parents comes from a heart that is in the right place: You want the family to know their child has been abused. But you don't know the whole story.

If you make that call, can you guarantee that child's safety? The true dynamics of a household are alien to you—even if you've known the family forever. Even if your kids are in the same class at school. Even if you like them a lot. Your disclosure could mean that child would return home to an even worse situation, complete with embarrassed parents or a furious sibling. Your well-intentioned telling could mean more risk for an already trapped child.

Your child may come to you with information that one of their friends is being abused, because children most often tell their peers about abuse. When a child talks about abuse to your child, keep in mind that over 90 percent of sexual abuse allegations are true.[lv]

Instead of calling the parents or gossiping to others, report the allegations of abuse. Show compassion to your child and to their friend if they have disclosed the abuse to you. Thank them for letting you know, and report the abuse using the channels provided by law enforcement and family protection agencies.

If the Predator is Your Child

If the predator is your minor child, refer to the in-depth information in Part 2 Chapter 8: Peers, for specific recommendations. Remember that juvenile predators may themselves be victims of neglect, abuse, or violence. Be open about any family issues, including any suspicions of abuse you have or were reported to you over the years about this child.

Protecting your child means getting them the help they need. If you're confused or unsure, contact a child advocacy professional or the Darkness to Light helpline for assistance. Call on a professional to intervene in sexual behaviors, instead of sweeping it under the rug. There are agencies working with families all across this country to educate and prevent further harm. See the Appendix for specifics.

The Message

Throughout this book, I repeatedly urge you to report abuse. Experts estimate that only a third of all child sexual abuse is reported, and statistics indicate that of those reported, half are screened out. Digest that for a

CREATING FORCE FIELD COMMUNITIES 197

second: Most sexual predators are not reported, investigated, or charged, which means that most sex offenders are unknown, not on any list. You may think that this mediocre track record of investigation and prosecution means that there is no point in reporting sex abuse cases. But the opposite is true: If we don't start reporting these crimes diligently, our society can't effectively respond. If most abusers know they will face no real consequences for abusing, they face no real deterrent to continuing to ruin people's lives by assaulting children.

Police and family protection agencies are the path to investigations and legal consequences. Encourage abuse survivors to document their experience and report it to the authorities, even if time has passed.

CONCLUSION

A SAFER FUTURE

Child sexual abuse survivors suffer even after the active abuse ends. Survivors of child sexual abuse are at greater risk for substance abuse, medical problems, mental illness, and sexual assaults in adulthood. Society at large suffers as well. According to the CDC, recent studies estimate $9.3 billion (about $29 per person in the US) a year is spent in victimization-related expenditures.[lvii]

Adults on the lookout for predators are real-life superheroes who help keep children safe and stop cycles of abuse and suffering that can last a lifetime. We also need to look at policies and laws surrounding children and sexual contact and push for reforms that make children's world safer.

Abolish Child Marriage

In the US, sexual activity is legal after the child reaches the age of consent. Any sexual activity with a person under the age of 16 is automatically categorized as coerced, forced, or unwanted, since a child is incapable of consenting.

There are some specific exceptions to this law, like when two underaged minors are involved, when parents give consent, or when religious waivers are approved. Absurdly, child marriage is legal in 44 states. Nine states have no minimum age for marriage. Nearly 300,000 children were legally married in the US between 2000 and 2018. [lviii]

Spending millions of dollars and staff hours fighting child predators online or in person while permitting a child, who otherwise has no ability to consent, to become married makes absolutely no sense. Child marriage is child sex abuse. Most child marriages are between older men and minor girls. We cannot combat child sexual abuse without prohibiting, on a state and federal level, child sexual abuse through marriage.

Speak Courageously

The silence of untold truths gives predators power. Instead of looking the other way and moving along after encountering a grooming predator, take the opportunity to shine a light that disinfects the disease of sex abuse. That disease weakens our families and communities, so draw attention to it every chance you get.

Identify and recognize grooming patterns, and stand up against predators—not just sometimes, but every time. Any family who shrugs and says "that wasn't really abuse," "we don't need this inconvenience," or "we'll just keep this to ourselves" makes all families vulnerable.

If you hit obstacles after reporting abuse, such as a legal battle over custody lost to an abuser, be ready to keep up the fight to do whatever is possible to advocate for your child's safety. At the very least, reporting the abuser and following up with protective legal action puts the predator's behavior under increased scrutiny, perhaps reducing the likelihood that the abuse will continue.

Be the Safety Zone for Your Child

If your child has been abused, part of the road ahead is helping them heal. Give them your complete support while they experience the safety and relief of having been released from the predator's trap of secrecy and threats. Most importantly, your child should know that you believe them, that they are not at fault in any way, and that you are completely committed to the fight for their protection.

Leave Abusive Families

Caring adults who listen, believe, and defend a child against an abuser risk losing their family. But for the safety of your child, you must be willing to completely remove a predator from your life. Many adults, possibly generations in a family, keep predators around rather than risk exploding the relationships. But relatives willing to harm your child through their denial or inaction lose all standing to participate in the family network. Have no contact with family members who encourage you to "try again" or look past the "incident." Any family devious enough to protect a predator while hanging a child out to dry is worth losing. Stay strong and focused on preventing further damage to your child.

Report Information

Local, state, and federal agencies are only as strong as the information they are provided. Promote and encourage your close family and friends to report any child sexual abuse they become aware of. If abuse goes unreported, predators go unchecked. Survivors go unheard. Everyone goes unprotected.

Take it to Court

Families who seek legal consequences for a child abuser should know that the process is often long and punishing. The legal system is not equipped to preserve the mental, spiritual, or physical well-being of child abuse survivors or their families. The use of legal sidelining, nondisclosure agreements, and backroom legal deals can disempower survivors. Many families learn too late in the legal process that the quality of a defense team, fierceness of a prosecutor, and cost of representation influence a case's outcome. Some tips to survive it include arming yourself with a strong legal representative, exploring both criminal and civil charges, focusing on the goal of legal consequences, and remembering that legal action is the best tool available, albeit punishing all involved.

Be a Champion for Child Safety

You are your child's greatest chance to avoid a predator. Take measures every day to protect your children by championing policies and practices that enforce safety for children and adults. Encourage families to call out grooming behaviors. Celebrate courageous members of your family and community who take a stand against predators. When issues arise, prioritize child safety above all else.

You've got the cherished job of shepherding this innocent spirit through childhood and adolescence to their bright future. You are not powerless against predators. Own your boldness by putting your child's safety first.

Encourage Sexual Health

Sexuality is complex and matures over a lifetime. As defined by the World Health Organization, sexual health is a state of physical, emotional, mental, and social well-being. Being a sexually healthy adult means enjoying a healthier body, a satisfying intimate life, positive relationships, and peace of mind.

Trustworthy sexual relationships can only form after people reach the age of consent, and often even later. Preventing child sexual abuse means a child gains the necessary time to understand intimacy and physical contact.

Never Permit Social Status to Eclipse Child Safety

Our social networks are wonderful when all parties respect shared standards for right and wrong, but the status quo can be catastrophic if a sexual predator is stalking children in our circles.

Adults don't want to implode friendships or possibly jeopardize someone's career or home life. We fear being perceived as untrusting or judgmental. We want to see the best in others, and we often rationalize or explain away abusive behavior. "I couldn't possibly make that accusation" is a frequent reaction.

When we experience the jolt of finding out that someone, an adult or minor, has groomed or abused our child, we may face a lose-lose situation. Staying quiet means you fail to defend your child, invalidate their experience of being violated, and do nothing to protect your community. And if you raise a flag and make a stink, you lose a friend, create tension in a neighborhood, and threaten family stability. It's a paralyzing choice. Predators who have ingratiated themselves into your life gradually pressure you to grant them more freedom with your child. Friends of the family may lean on you to let their child spend more time with them. And it can be easy to subjugate children's needs when an adult family member is insisting on their own agenda and making you feel guilty about refusing. All of these people disparage your safety protocols as fear and paranoia, and you sometimes bend those rules in the spirit of keeping the adult relationship on solid footing.

But if grooming behaviors and abuse occur, staying silent isn't one of your available options. It's no longer a workable option to ignore what has happened. Yes, there will be an impact on you socially and emotionally, but you are not at fault for that. The fault lies solely with the predator. I'd like to tell you that you are imagining the lose-lose situation posed by the discovery and reporting of child sex abuse, that there is nothing to fear, and that there is a way to avoid both of those problem scenarios. But I cannot.

One of my primary reasons for writing this book, however, is to help you avoid ever getting to that point. The two most successful ways to do that are to recognize and deter predatory behavior long before any sexual contact occurs and to profoundly shift how our society responds to allegations of abuse. Accomplishing both those things means that children are safer, communities are stronger, and families are supported by society at large.

Remember, you are the architect of the force field around your child—not your friends, not your relatives, and not the recreation league coach. Don't let your fear of disrupting those relationships and upending your life distract you from your priority of keeping your children safe.

Pass This Book On

Don't wait for someone else to protect children where you live. You can do this right now. Give this book away to someone else: your mother, a coworker, your brother, your friend from the gym, your neighbor. Begin the conversation about grooming today to start making the world safer for all our children tomorrow.

i   Department of Justice, Office of Justice Programs, Bureau of Justice Statistics, Sexual Assault of Young Children as Reported to Law Enforcement (2000).

ii   United States Department of Health and Human Services, Administration for Children and Families, Administration on Children, Youth and Families, Children's Bureau. Child Maltreatment Survey. Exhibit 5-2 Selected Maltreatment Types by Perpetrator's Sex. Page 65. (2013).

iii   Leeb RT, Paulozzi L, Melanson C, et al. Child maltreatment surveillance: uniform definitions for public health and recommended data elements, version 1.0. Centers for Disease Control and Prevention, National Center for Injury Prevention and Control; Atlanta (GA): 2008.

iv   United States Age of Consent Laws By State, https://www.ageofconsent.net/states, 01/20/2022

v   Finkelhor, D. & Ormrod, R. Characteristics of crimes against juveniles. Juvenile Justice Bulletin - NCJ179034. (pgs. 1-11). Washington, DC: US Government Printing Office.

vi   Department of Justice, Office of Justice Programs, Bureau of Justice Statistics, Sexual Assault of Young Children as Reported to Law Enforcement (2000). https://bjs.ojp.gov/content/pub/pdf/saycrle.pdf

vii   Department of Justice, Office of Justice Programs, Bureau of Justice Statistics, Sexual Assault of Young Children as Reported to Law Enforcement (2000). https://bjs.ojp.gov/content/pub/pdf/saycrle.pdf

viii   American Psychiatric Association. (2013a). Diagnostic and Statistical Manual of Mental Disorders. (5th Edition). Washington, DC.

ix   RAINN Statistics, https://www.rainn.org/statistics/children-and-teens, 01/12/2022

x   Snyder, H. "Sexual Assault of Young Children as Reported to Law Enforcement: Victim, Incident, and Offender Characteristics." Bureau of Justice Statistics, U.S. Department of Justice, 2000

xi   Townsend, C., Rheingold, A., Haviland, M.L. (2016). Estimating a child sexual abuse prevalence rate for practitioners: An updated review of child sexual abuse prevalence studies. Charleston SC: Darkness to Light. Retrieved from www.D2L.org/1in10.

xii   London, K., Bruck, M., Ceci, S. J., & Shuman, D. W. (2005). Disclosure of Child Sexual Abuse: What Does the Research Tell Us About the Ways That Children Tell? Psychology, Public Policy, and Law, 11(1), 194–226. https://doi.org/10.1037/1076-8971.11.1.194

xiii   de Becker, Gavin. The Gift of Fear. Bloomsbury Publishing PLC, 2000

xiv   Finkelhor, D., Ormrod,R., Chaffin, M. (2009) Juveniles who commit sex offenses against minors. Juvenile Justice Bulletin, OJJDP, Office of Justice Programs

xv   Albert, D. et al. "Peer Influences on Adolescent Decision Making." Current directions in psychological science vol. 22,2 (2013): 114-120. doi:10.1177/0963721412471347

xvi   https://www.uscourts.gov/sites/default/files/68_3_5_0.pdf , 02/04/2022

xvii   Vandiver, D. M, and G. Kercher. "Offender and victim characteristics of registered female sexual offenders in Texas: a proposed typology of female sexual offenders." Sexual abuse: a journal of research and treatment vol. 16,2 (2004): 121-37. doi:10.1177/107906320401600203

xviii   https://ojp.gov/pdffiles1/ojjdp/214383.pdf, 02/29/2022

xix   https://bjs.ojp.gov/content/pub/pdf/saycrle.pdf

xx   https://bjs.ojp.gov/content/pub/pdf/saycrle.pdf

xxi   https://bjs.gov/content/pub/pdf/saycrle.pdf

xxii   Vandiver, D. M. "Female sex offenders: a comparison of solo offenders and co-offenders." Violence and victims vol. 21,3 (2006): 339-54. doi:10.1891/vivi.21.3.339

xxiii   Cortoni, F. et al. "The Proportion of Sexual Offenders Who Are Female Is Higher Than Thought." Criminal Justice and Behavior 44 (2017): 145 - 162.

xxiv   Tozdan, S. et al. "Uncovering Female Child Sexual Offenders-Needs and Challenges for Practice and Research." Journal of clinical medicine vol. 8,3 401. 22 Mar. 2019, doi:10.3390/jcm8030401

xxv   Finkelhor, D.; Ormrod, R. and Chaffin, M. Juveniles who commit sex offenses against minors. Juvenile Justice Bulletin – NCJ227763 (1-12pgs). Washington, DC: US Government Printing Office.

xxvi   Porn sites attract more visitors than Netflix, Amazon and Twitter combined (dnaindia.com), 01/24.2022

xxvii   Children_and_Pornography_Factsheet-Updated-2020.pdf(digitalkidsinitiative.com), 01/24/2022

xxviii   The average age for a child getting their first smartphone is now 10.3 years | TechCrunch, 01/24/2022

xxix   Let's Talk About Porn. Is It As Harmless As Society Says It Is? (fightthenewdrug.org), 01/24/2022

xxx   Wright, P. J., & Tokunaga, R. S. (2016). Men's Objectifying Media Consumption, Objectification of Women, and Attitudes Supportive of Violence Against Women. Archives of sexual behavior, 45(4), 955–964. https://doi.org/10.1007/s10508-015-0644-8

xxxi   Bridges AJ, Wosnitzer R, Scharrer E, Sun C, Liberman R. Aggression and sexual behavior in best-selling pornography videos: a content analysis update. Violence Against Women. 2010 Oct;16(10):1065-85. doi: 10.1177/1077801210382866. PMID: 20980228.

xxxii   Posting About Your Kids Online Could Damage Their Futures (forbes.com), 01/24/2022

xxxiii   Snyder, H. "Sexual Assault of Young Children as Reported to Law Enforcement: Victim, Incident, and Offender Characteristics." Bureau of Justice Statistics, U.S. Department of Justice, 2000

xxxiv   Teens Spend 'Astounding' Nine Hours a Day in Front of Screens: Researchers | WVEA, 01/24/2022

xxxv   https://mandatedreporter.com/blog/how-long-does-a-mandated-reporter-have-to-report-child-abuse, 07/06/2021

xxxvi   Snyder, H. N. (2000). Sexual assault of young children as reported to law enforcement: Victim, incident, and offender characteristics. Washington, DC: U.S. Department of Justice, Office of Justice Programs, Bureau of Justice Statistics. http://www.ojp.usdoj.gov/bjs/pub/pdf/saycrle.pdf

xxxvii   Tracy, N. (2021, December 17). Effects of Child Sexual Abuse on Children, HealthyPlace. Retrieved on 2022, January 25 from https://www.healthyplace.com/abuse/child-sexual-abuse/effects-of-child-sexual-abuse-on-children

xxxviii   Finkelhor, D., Ormrod,R., Chaffin, M. (2009) Juveniles who commit sex offenses against minors. Juvenile Justice Bulletin, OJJDP, Office of Justice Programs

xxxix   https://www.d2l.org/wp-content/uploads/2017/01/Statistics_5_Consequences.pdf

xl   U.S. has world's highest rate of children living in single-parent households | Pew Research Center, 01/25/2022

xli   https://www.verywellfamily.com/single-parent-census-data-2997668

xlii   https://www.verywellfamily.com/single-parent-census-data-2997668

xliii   Sedlak, A., et al. Fourth National Incidence Study of Child Abuse and Neglect (NIS–4). U.S. Department of Health and Human Services, Administration for Children and Families, 2010, p. 16, acf.hhs.gov/sites/default/files/documents/opre/nis4_report_congress_full_pdf_jan2010.pdf.

xliv   Sedlak, A., et al. Fourth National Incidence Study of Child Abuse and Neglect (NIS–4). U.S. Department of Health and Human Services, Administration for Children and Families, 2010, p. 16, acf.hhs.gov/sites/default/files/documents/opre/nis4_report_congress_full_pdf_jan2010.pdf.

xlv   https://lifesaving.com/issues-safety-rescue/bathtub-drownings-beware-of-the-hazards-and-risks-to-young-children/, 09/03/2022

xlvi   The average age for a child getting their first smartphone is now 10.3 years | TechCrunch, 01/24/2022

xlvii   The Common-Sense Census: Media Use by Tweens and Teens, 2019 | Common Sense Media, 02/07/2022

xlviii   https://www.fastcompany.com/1687648/whos-texting-your-kids-class-66-time-parents, 04/13/2022

xlix   2019_SOP_National_Final.pdf (aspeninstitute.org), 02/08/2022

l   Lack of Presence For Female Coaches Extends to Kids' Games (forbes.com), 02/08/2022

li   Youth sports study: Declining participation, rising costs and unqualified coaches - The Washington Post , 08/03/2022

lii   S.534 - 115th Congress (2017-2018): Protecting Young Victims from Sexual Abuse and Safe Sport Authorization Act of 2017 | Congress.gov | Library of Congress

liii   Sedlak, A.J., Mettenburg, J., Basena, M., Petta, I., McPherson, K., Greene, A., & Li, S. (2010). Fourth National Incidence Study of Child Abuse and Neglect (NIS–4): Report to Congress, Executive Summary. Washington, DC: U.S. Department of Health and Human Services, Administration for Children and Families.

liv   Child Maltreatment 2020 (hhs.gov) , 1/23/2022

lv   Everson, M., & Boat, B. (1989). False allegations of sexual abuse by children and adolescents.Journal of the American Academy of Child and Adolescent Psychiatry. 28, 2:230-35.

lvi   London, K., Bruck, M., Ceci, S., & Shuman, D. (2003) Disclosure of child sexual abuse: What does the research tell us about the ways that children tell? Psychology, Public Policy, and Law, 11(1), 194-226.

lvii   Letourneau, E. J et al. "The economic burden of child sexual abuse in the United States." Child abuse & neglect vol. 79 (2018): 413-422. doi:10.1016/j.chiabu.2018.02.020

lviii   United States' Child Marriage Problem: Study Findings (April 2020) - Unchained At Last

lix   United States' Child Marriage Problem: Study Findings (April 2020) - Unchained At Last, https://www.unchainedatlast.org/laws-to-end-child-marriage/, 02/22/2022

lx   https://www.who.int/health-topics/sexual-health#tab=tab_1, 1/24/2022

APPENDIX

Resources

Center for Missing and Exploited Children – www.missingkids.org/
Darkness to Light - www.d2l.org/
ChildHelp - www.childhelp.org/ Hotline or Text 1(800) 422-4453
Stop It Now - www.stopitnow.org

Treatment of Sexual Abusers Research

ATSA - www.atsa.com
Sexual Abuse: A Journal of Research and Treatment, published by Sage

Signs of Suicidality

National Suicide Crisis Line - Text or Call 988

TALKING ABOUT:
Wanting to die
Great guilt or shame
Being a burden to others

FEELING:
Empty, hopeless, trapped, or having no reason to live
Extremely sad, more anxious, agitated, or full of rage
Unbearable emotional or physical pain

CHANGING BEHAVIOR, SUCH AS:
Making a plan or researching ways to die
Withdrawing from friends, saying good bye, or giving away important items
Taking dangerous risks such as driving extremely fast
Displaying extreme mood swings
Eating or sleeping more or less
Using drugs or alcohol more often

If these warning signs apply to you or someone you know, get help as soon as possible, particularly if the behavior is new or has increased recently. (Source www.nimh.nih.gov/suicideprevention)

Signs of Child Sexual Abuse

EMOTIONAL SIGNS
Emotional and behavioral signs or changes are more common than physical signs and can include:
• Anxiety and depression
• Sleep disturbances, including nightmares or night terrors
• Change in eating habits
• Unusual fear of certain people or places; reluctance to be alone with a certain person
• Changes in mood that could including anger, aggressiveness towards parents, siblings, friends, pets
• Rebellion or withdrawal; runaway behavior
• Change in attitude towards school or academic performance; lack of interest in friends, sports, or other activities
• Unexplained or frequent health problems like headaches or stomach aches
• Poor self-esteem; avoidance of relationships
• Self-mutilation or change in body perception, like thinking of self or body as dirty or bad; suicidal thoughts
• Regression to previously outgrown behaviors, for example, bedwetting or thumb sucking
• Abnormal sexual behaviors or knowledge of advanced sexual language and behaviors
• Too "perfect" behavior or overly compliant behavior

PHYSICAL SIGNS OF ABUSE
Direct physical signs of sexual abuse are not common. However, when physical signs are present, they may include bruising, bleeding, redness and bumps, or scabs around the mouth, genital, or anus. Urinary tract infections, sexually transmitted diseases, and abnormal vaginal or penile discharge are also warning signs.

There are other indirect physical signs that include:
• Persistent or recurring pain during urination or bowel movements
• Wetting or soiling accidents unrelated to toilet training
• Sexually transmitted diseases

- Chronic stomach pain
- Headaches

(Source Identifying Child Sexual Abuse - Darkness to Light (d2l.org))

Family Safety Plan

To begin your Family Safety Plan, evaluate each of these questions on behalf of each child in your household before any activity. If one is unanswered, the child does not participate or needs to get more information. If an answer doesn't sit well with you, rethink how the event can take place by altering the logistics.

Who: Who will be supervising? Will they be alone or with another adult? Who will be attending? Will there be younger siblings, older siblings, additional family members present? Will there be additional adults present? Who can the child go to at the event for immediate attention or care? Who can the child contact to reach you while at the activity?

What: What is the activity or event? Does the activity align with your family values? Is everyone attending directly participating in the activity? If children are not directly participating, how will they occupy themselves productively? Who will supervise the children not participating? What happens if an adult changes the plan spontaneously, without your permission? How will you address that adult in future planning?

Where: Where does the event or activity take place? Will there be a venue change, if so, where to? Are parents permitted to supervise, observe, or attend? Does the activity venue come with adult supervisors? Do you entrust those adults with the wellbeing of your child? What policies for safety are present at the activity or event space?

When: When will it take place? For how long? Daytime or nighttime hours? If overnight, what are the measures in place for safety and prevention? What concessions are needed for the child to be away for that length of time (such as menstrual products, overnight pants, diapers, beloved object from home, etc.)

How: How will the child get to and from the activity? With whom? What communication method would you like your child or the supervising adult to use to reach you? In case of emergency, how will the child be reunited with family?

212 **DUCK DUCK GROOM**

Why: Why is participating in this event or activity important? What will my child learn or experience that will move them closer to our family values? Who is pushing for my child to attend, myself, my child, or another person? Why would that individual be so motivated to include my child?

Upon reviewing your answers to your Family Safety Plan, you're equipped to make a decision about whether your child will attend. You have the authority to restrict or permit any access to your child at any time for any reason. Furthermore, you're never obligated to provide a reason if your child does not participate. A simple, "unfortunately, my child won't be able to make it," will suffice.

Questions for Caregivers

In addition to completing a background check, reference checks and follow through, and basic information, such as address, school, phone number, social security number, and date of birth, use the questions below to get you started in your in-person interview of the candidate. You may not need all questions, but directly addressing these topics will strengthen your decision when hiring caregivers.

What draws you to work with children?

What are your strengths in working with children?

What are your biggest challenges when working with children? What situations are most difficult?

How do you discipline a misbehaving child?

How do you handle your device when in the presence of children? Photo or video taking and sharing? Are children permitted to use or watch along with you on your device?

How would you handle a child who shares they are being abused by a family member or friend?

How do you handle private spaces for bathing or toileting? What is your expectation when washing, dressing, or toileting my child?

How would you handle a child who is touching themselves on their genitals in your presence?

What are your thoughts about having guests over while you're babysitting?

Share with me a circumstance where you've had to withhold information from a child's parent? Tell me about any circumstance where you had a secret with a child you cared for?

Please describe a time when babysitting did not go well. Why? Looking back, what could you have done to improve the outcome?